Advance Praise

"*Ragás, because the sea has no place to grab is tne documentation of the 'homecoming' of a mother and a daughter to Cabo Verde, and to the possibilities of themselves, the encounter with family members, who they had never met or had not seen for more than four decades. These two dimensions brought them to a (dis)comfort that made them realize that the vibrant silence of memories unveiled would actually trigger a sense of personal and historical growth and appeasement. It is a journey that anyone can identify with, as it sparks the universal feeling of the need to both embrace our roots and to nurture our own paths." —**Carla Fernandes**, journalist, host of Rádio Afrolis, and founder of Afrolis Cultural Association

"*Ragás* is an amazing text that breaks the silence of thousands of lives whose mental and social life was disrupted, distorted by colonial violence and Portuguese hegemonic history. More importantly, it is a story of love and resistance, revivified tracks, a living bouquet of herstory, which escapes from the prison of biography and offers wonderful paths for our diaspora in Portugal and beyond to walk as we reorganize the foreclosures of memory by official narratives, and become protagonists once more." —**Flávio "LBC Soldjah" Ze-nun Almada**, emcee/rapper, writer, and general coordinator of Associação Cultural Moinho da Juventude at Cova da Moura

"It is often said that 'memory is the key to liberation,' but what happens when memory is dormant, suppressed, misplaced, seemingly lost? How do we search for what has no form? Maria Isabel Vaz and Sónia Vaz Borges' *Ragás, because the sea has no place to grab* is a clear meditation on this process. A thesis on unpacking and mapping a living archive." —**James Pope**, Associate Professor of Africana Studies, Winston-Salem State University and founding director of Educational Initiatives for Africa World Now Project

"I can think of no other work that provides such deep insight into the lived intimacies of the afterlives of national liberation struggles and their diasporas. *Ragás, because the sea has no place to grab* is to be savored in stillness, discussed in study groups with comrades, and taught in classrooms where militant education for home-grown anticolonial liberation remains on the syllabus."—**Jodi Melamed**, author of *Represent and Destroy: Rationalizing Violence in the New Racial Capitalism*

"*Ragás, because the sea has no place to grab* provides a beautiful and deeply felt memoir of migration, diaspora, belonging, and returning home. Maria Isabel Vaz and Sónia Vaz Borges bring us along on the intimate journey they take together back to Cabo Verde, a homecoming after forty-two years as complex and emotional as one could imagine. This book provides rich personal insights into the paradoxes of memory and the legacies of colonial histories and traumas. It is a must read for those interested in learning more about the innermost and constant struggles that hinder individual and collective liberation across time and space in the African diaspora." —**Keisha-Khan Perry**, Presidential Penn Compact Associate Professor of Africana Studies, University of Pennsylvania

"Situated at the precipice between history and memory, *Ragás, because the sea has no place to grab* brings the reader into everyday life in Cabo Verde. The worlds women build through community become tangible and visceral through the portal of mother-daughter travel. This book is an unforgettable journey." —**Robyn C. Spencer-Antoine**, Associate Professor of History and African American Studies, Wayne State University

"This work is both a declaration of love and a generous and rare testimony in the first person of the contemporary Black experience between Cabo Verde and Portugal. As mother and daughter set off on this fascinating journey of 'return' to their 'root,' they know that no one ever truly goes back anywhere—and that in the harshness of women's (post)colonial lives, there is no place for romanticization. It is both a search for themselves and each other that they have embarked on, traversing a sea of memories and affections. Continuing the work Sónia Vaz Borges began with *Na Pó do Spera* (2014), but with a newfound and moving intimacy, *Ragás, because the sea has no place to grab* also provides a personal insight into the network of affections behind *Militant Education, Liberation Struggle, Consciousness, The PAIGC Education in Guinea Bissau 1963–1978* (2019). A must-read for anyone interested in the resistance and resignification of belonging through an Afro-Portuguese prism." —**Cristina Roldão**, Professor of ESE-IPS and researcher of CIES-IUL – Instituto Universitário de Lisboa

RAGÁS, BECAUSE THE SEA
HAS NO PLACE TO GRAB

RAGÁS, BECAUSE THE SEA HAS NO PLACE TO GRAB
A memoir of home, migration, and African liberation

Maria Isabel Vaz
Sónia Vaz Borges

Brooklyn, NY
Philadelphia, PA
commonnotions.org

Ragás, because the sea has no place to grab:
A memoir of home, migration, and African liberation

© 2024 Maria Isabel Vaz and Sónia Vaz Borges
This edition © 2024 Common Notions

This is work is licensed under the Creative Commons Attribution-NonCommercial 4.0 International. To view a copy of this license, visit https://creativecommons.org/licenses/by-nc/4.0/

ISBN: 978-1-945335-09-9 | eBook ISBN: 978-1-945335-22-8
Library of Congress Number: 2024937149
10 9 8 7 6 5 4 3 2 1

Common Notions
c/o Interference Archive
314 7th St.
Brooklyn, NY 11215

Common Notions
c/o Making Worlds Bookstore
210 S. 45th St.
Philadelphia, PA 19104

www.commonnotions.org
info@commonnotions.org

Discounted bulk quantities of our books are available for organizing, educational, or fundraising purposes. Please contact Common Notions at the address above for more information.

Special thanks to Jethro Souter for editorial support.

Cover design by Josh MacPhee
Layout design and typesetting by Suba Murugan

ABOUT THE NONALIGNED SERIES

Nonaligned is dedicated to fiction, literary nonfiction, and poetry that explores the historical and ongoing legacies of anticolonial politics, the evolving nature of imperialism, and the world-making freedom movements of our times. The series highlights vital and creative sources of internationalist imagination within the fractures and faultlines of the current world order. The name takes inspiration from the worldwide anticolonial and anti-imperialist self-determination movements that sparked a wave of decolonization in the 1960s and '70s across Africa, Latin America, Asia, and the Arab world.

In the Nonaligned Series

Daughter, Son, Assassin, Steven Salaita, 9781945335082
Ragás, because the sea has no place to grab, Maria Isabel Vaz and Sónia Vaz Borges, 9781945335099
Rojava: A Novel of Kurdish Freedom, Sharam Qawami (translated by Kiyoumars Zamani), 9781945335105

"We must dare to be critical of our urge to tell our stories, of the ways we tell them . . . . One must write and one must have time to write. Having time to write, time to wait through silences, time to go to the pen and paper or the typewriter when the breakthrough finally comes."

—bell hooks

With and for my mother, for helping and allowing me to write and publish these pages, stories, and memories.

Ilha de santiago [Santiago Island], Cabo Verde

MAP INFORMATION

1. Praia city
2. São Francisco Beach
3. Cidade Velha
4. Fonte de Almeida
5. Milho Branco
6. Rui Vaz
7. Monte Negro
8. Santiago – Pedra Badejo
9. João Teves
10. Lage
11. Assomada
12. Jalalo Ramos
13. Serra Malagueta
14. Calheta de São Miguel
15. Ribeira da Prata
16. Chão Bom
17. Tarrafal

CONTENTS

Foreword   xvii

Prologue   xxi

One | Bia d'Lulucha   1

Two | From Amadora to Praia   7

Three | Cabo Verde   11

Four | Eugénio Lima   15

Five | Pelourinho da Praia   19

Six | Assomada – Cutelo   23

Seven | Monte Negro   29

Eight | Tchada Leitão – Jalalo Ramos   33

Nine | Tungiasis – Sand Flea   41

Ten | Gelo André   43

Eleven | Childhood memories   47

Twelve | Cidade Velha   49

Thirteen | Tarrafal   53

Fourteen | Newspaper – *Jornal Voz di Povo*   61

Fifteen | Quintal do Burro   65

Sixteen | João Teves   67

Seventeen Praying mantis   71

Eighteen | Lage   75

Nineteen | Retelling the story   81

Twenty | Fonte de Almeida   85

Twenty-one | Her body and my scars   89

Twenty-two | The hitch-hike   93

Twenty-three | Mantenhas para Casa   99

Twenty-four | Together with the Freedom Fighters   103

Twenty-five | Departures   111

Twenty-six | An abiding memory:
     Santiago – Pedra Badejo   115

Twenty-seven | Unwelcome travel companions   117

Twenty-eight | Ragás   123

About the Authors   129

About Common Notions   131

FOREWORD

During their trip to Cabo Verde, Dona Maria Isabel Vaz warns Sónia Vaz Borges to respect the sea, *"pamodi mar, ka ten kau di pega."* ["Respect the sea, because the sea has no place to grab."]

Ragás, the story of that trip, is a search for where history, personal and public, has places to grab. Dona Isabel had left the islands for Portugal decades earlier, and never returned. Sónia, her daughter, had never been there, but had heard stories, or parts of stories—had heard names of relatives. Much of Sónia's life and work in Portugal had taken place among Cabo Verdeans, speaking Kriolo, dancing and singing popular songs; later organizing and studying Cabo Verdeans in Portugal, and eventually studying the African Party for the Independence of Guinea Bissau and the Cape Verde (PAIGC) revolution itself. Hard-earned savings to do research on the revolution provided the wherewithal for daughter and mother to see Cabo Verde together.

As mother and daughter search for relatives, Sónia also looks for people who had been active in the PAIGC's revolutionary era–education program. The two searches run along similar paths and toward similar ends. Finding one person opens the way to meet three more, especially after an initial contact gains some trust in you and your project. For the research, person by person, trust opens the way to shared stories, photos, and other materials. On the familial side, some of the meetings seem more fraught, trust more fragile. There are still things that can't be said, stories that remain fragments, or words spoken very quietly, to be heard by only the immediate listener. There are things about the past some of us still can't speak about, or can't speak about in any sort of public space.

Reasons for silence vary: shame, guilt, protecting a loved one, and the ongoing pain of old traumas never fully healed. Four decades after independence, the traumas of the colonial period are not all healed. We see scene after scene of enormous emotional weight—family and friends seeing Dona Isabel for the first time in decades, and meeting her daughter for the first time ever. And often during those encounters there are things that still can't be said to Isabel or shared with Sónia.

The revolutionary educators Sónia interviews were trying to build a system that would free the hearts and minds of people in Guinea-Bissau and Cabo Verde of colonial ideas, values, and attachments. To what extent any of those educators thought of their work as healing, we can't say. But it is clear that emotional damage caused by Portuguese colonists and their system remains, and is particularly borne there by those of Isabel's generation and their elders.

In our world of the post-colonial and the de-colonial, many hope to find home, real home, in a return to the place from which family was forced to move, or practices they were forced to repress—a romantic idea of restoration. Sónia, who narrates the women's story, is wary that her own romantic ideas of a motherland will inter-fere with actually seeing what she encounters. Opposed to simple ideas of recovery or return, is the Pan-African tra-dition of seeing the past not as a point of arrival, but as a practice from which to build anew, along the way making real what Sid Lemelle and Robin Kelley called Imagining Home.

One of Sónia's realizations on the voyage is that home is in her mother's lap, or sitting on the floor in front of her mother's chair, head resting on her knees, or sharing a bed, or doing each other's hair. Home is made of re-lationships. During the journey, practical questions arise of who will still be alive, or who might have moved and be untraceable. But there are also questions, not so loud-ly voiced, of what sort of relationships will exist among those who are found, what to do and how to feel.

The processes of discovering who's around and of beginning to rebuild the relationships are done through networks of women and their work. Some of the ini-tial contacts are made through women in the market—sometimes prompted by a question, and other times by the shadow of familiarity transforming a stranger's face. Many of the reunions involve a meal, often with which-ever family and friends are still in the area, and in some cases Dona Isabel and Sónia, though also guests, work with other women in the kitchen preparing the meal.

To the extent that Dona Isabel and Sónia make their home in Cabo Verde, it is in relationships built through women's work—in the markets, the kitchens, and at the table. If Sónia finds home in her mother's lap, she and her mother discover it again at the kitchen table, doing the work that generations have done to sustain themselves, their families, and their neighbors.

Collective work—working towards survival pending revolution—is perhaps the handle that sea-tossed memory presents to the women? There are stories from the revolution that have been waiting for someone to bring them to light, and other stories, no less meaningful, that are only ever partly revealed. This latter kind of writing—about stories still too difficult to speak, to speak publicly, or to discuss after they have been told—radiantly fills these beautiful pages—the images and words showing us how memory differs, but is inseparable from history.

Craig Gilmore and Ruth Wilson Gilmore
May 24, 2023 New York City

PROLOGUE

"Rua Cidade de Amadora." We stumbled upon this street name one morning in Cabo Verde and burst out laughing: "City of Amadora Street." We were in Tarrafal, on the north coast of Santiago Island, on what was my mum's first trip back to her homeland in forty-two years, and my first ever visit. But looking at that street sign it was as if we'd gone all that way to end up back in Amadora, the city my parents moved to in their early twenties, where they built a house and raised five daughters, the city where I've lived my whole life.

For the uninitiated, Amadora is located just outside of Lisbon. It sits on one of the most well-known tourist trails in Portugal, but is very much not part of that trail. The train from Lisbon to Sintra, a UNESCO town with hilltop castles and fairytale palaces, passes through Amadora, though visitors rarely get off. It's not hard to distinguish the sightseers from the commuters, for this is the Linha de Sintra, the Sintra Line, LS in youth-speak, serving Lisbon's most densely-populated periphery neighborhoods. These neighborhoods collectively make up Amadora and are predominantly inhabited by African diaspora communities.

The history of these neighborhoods dates back to the late 1960s and tells the story of successive waves of migration. The first people to settle in the area were Portuguese migrants from the countryside who moved to Lisbon in search of better opportunities and living conditions. Unable to afford to buy a house or rent a room, they began to build shanty homes in abandoned wheat fields and vacant land. Family followed family, and with time the neighborhood grew. Then in the 1970s, as Portugal waged war in the colonized territories—Angola, Mozambique, and Guinea-Bissau—Portuguese settlers returned to Portugal, fleeing war or the "decolonization" process. With nowhere else to go, many set up home in Amadora and continued the building process. There were some Africans living in the neighborhood back then—especially migrant worker men—but it was in the late 1980s when this segment really boomed. The Portuguese population gradually began to move out and sell the land they'd built on, land they did not in fact own, to the new arrivals from Africa. Today most of Amadora's self-built neighborhood inhabitants are Black Africans. The majority hail from Cabo Verde.[1]

The LS leaves Rossio station in downtown Lisbon and calls at Benfica, home to the famous football team, before leaving the city limits. The next stop is Damaia where, on the hill to the left, sits Bairro Cova da Moura, a so-called "clandestine" neighborhood that has resisted repeated government proposals to demolish it. To the right is Bair-

---

1. Sónia Vaz Borges, *Na Pó di Spéra. Percursos nos bairros da Estrada Militar, Santa Filomena e da Encosta Nascente*, Fundação Calouste Gulbenkian/Principia, 2014.

ro da Damaia, which has been less fortunate. The target
of a PER Special Rehousing Program (*Programa Especial
de Realojamento* in Portuguese), it is slowly being gutted
to death, its community displaced. The same fate has already befallen Bairro Estrela de Africa and Bairro 6 de
Maio, just down the tracks at the next station, Reboleira. Both areas have been reduced to rubble and become a
waste ground, aside from one or two homes housing the
last holdouts. Slipping through the PER net, they're stuck
in limbo, reliant on the kindness of strangers and aid
from local NGOs. I grew up in Reboleira, but on the other
side of the tracks, and top of the hill, literally if not met-
aphorically. Like Cova de Moura, our section of informal
housing has somehow survived. The next station is Amadora itself, flanked by the Centro Comercial Babilónia, a
shopping mall that opened in 1984 and featured a tiny
store selling chocolate croissants, and the now closed cin-
ema room, the highlight of my school days. Next comes
Queluz-Belas, but before arriving there, on the right is
what remains of the Bairro de Santa Filomena, Bairro da
Estrada Militar, and Bairro Ponte de Carenque communities, all now hollowed out. After Queluz-Belas, the landscape changes: the tourists can start admiring other dense
architectonical views of the vertical periphery.

Growing up, these neighborhoods were like islands
in many ways, cut off from the rest of the city and sepa-
rated from each other by hillsides, main roads, and train
tracks. Thus, Amadora was a sort of archipelago of African diasporas, another Cabo Verde, if you will.

Cape Verde in English; *Cabo Verde* in Portuguese, and
now as it should be officially written; *Kau Verd* in Kriolu,
the common tongue—gets its name from the green cape

on Senegal's coast, the nearest strip of mainland. As an archipelago in the middle of the Atlantic Ocean, it is a place of strategic geopolitical importance. The US has long sought to establish a military base there, similar to the one it maintained in the Azores. But despite this, Cabo Verde is often conspicuous by its absence on maps.

Subject to long dry seasons, the islands can suffer from severe droughts, and have historically been plagued by famine. The rainy season, known as Azáguas, is always eagerly anticipated. In the blink of an eye, the dusty, brown landscape transforms into a multitude of greens and, in the good years, dams are filled. The rain also sees the islands come to life: it's time to prepare the fields and to plant. Subsistence farming is still a major element of the Cabo Verdean economy.

The population of Cabo Verde stands at a little over half a million, spread over four thousand square kilometers and spanning ten islands. The islands are divided into two groups according to the wind direction: the Sotavento (Leeward) islands, which is the northern group, comprising Brava, Fogo, Santiago, and Maio; and the Barlavento (Windward), the southern group, featuring Santo Antão, São Vicente, São Nicolau, Santa Luzia, Sal, and Boa Vista.

Santiago is the largest and most prominent island, home to the capital city, Praia. It is also where my entire family comes from, at least in so far as we know, and as far back as we can trace. Santiago was where Portuguese sailors first settled, establishing what is now called *Cidade Velha* (Old City) in 1460. Colonialism and slavery followed, and independence was achieved in 1975 under the leadership of the PAIGC, the African Party for the Independence of Guinea Bissau and Cape Verde (the *Partido*

Africano para a Independência da Guiné e Cabo Verde in Portuguese).

Unlike Amadora, tourists do come to the islands, and tourism is one of the main economic sectors for Cabo Verde, or the Morabeza Islands, as they are sometimes marketed, to cash in on the country's international music reputation. But while visitors come to the islands to relax, explore, and indulge themselves, Cabo Verdeans themselves are forced to migrate, first and foremost to the urban centers, and then abroad. The expat Cabo Verdean population is likely larger than the population of the Cabo Verdean islands.

But migration is nothing new for Cabo Verde, indeed it's ingrained in island history. The colonial settlers were migrants after all, then came the forced migration of the Atlantic Slave Trade, for which Cabo Verde became an important hub. Cabo Verdeans were regularly recruited as crew on nineteenth-century New England whaling ships. And so it went on, wave after wave of comings and goings, shaping the make-up of the current population, and giving each island its own culture and characteristics.

People like to joke that no matter where you go in the world, you'll find a Cabo Verdean living there. They get mistaken for Surinamese in the Netherlands, Somalis in Sweden[2] and "Some Kind of Funny Porto Rican" in the United States.[3] In Portugal, where most of the emigrant

---

2. Batalha, Luís, and Jørgen Carling, eds. *Transnational Archipelago: Perspectives on Cape Verdean Migration and Diaspora.* Amsterdam University Press, 2008, 3.
3. On Cabo Verdeans in the United States, see Claire Andrade-Watkins (dir.), "'Some Kind of Funny Porto Rican?': A Cape Verdean American Story" (2006 USA, 83 minutes, PBS 55" version online)

population resides, they are simply seen as Black, when not called the Portuguese N-word.

My parents were part of the emigration story, and I was part of that expat population. I'd gone to Cabo Verde to research the PAIGC's education programs, but I'd also unconsciously gone to explore my Cabo Verdean roots. And I'd gone with my mum to find out where she was from and how she'd respond to it. That street sign suggested you couldn't take either of us out of Amadora. But we'd soon see about that.

ONE

Bia d'Lulucha

The flights are booked—I'm going to Cabo Verde for the first time! But I'm not going alone. My mum, Maria Isabel Vaz, a woman everyone calls Bia d' Lulucha for some friends, or simply Dona Bia, is coming with me. Or maybe it's actually the other way around: maybe I'm going with her.

I've always wanted to go to Cabo Verde and see the places my mum and my dad, my aunties, uncles, and neighbors are forever telling stories about. It was just a matter of waiting for the right moment, and now that moment has come. I've got a big work project to do there, conducting research for my PhD, and I've also got the money to bring my mother with me. To be totally honest, I've got much more of an idea about what I'm doing regarding the former than the latter. It's now forty-two years since Bia left Cabo Verde, more specifically Santiago Island, and more specifically still, the Cutelo area of Santa Catarina province. She left with her parents and siblings when they all sailed to Portugal on a big boat. She has never been anywhere near an airplane, and her dream of one day returning to the land of her birth has always been just that, a dream. For a long time, life circumstances intervened and robbed her of every opportunity she had to go back, and then there was simply no money for such things. When

I told her I'd booked the flights, her reaction was more one of shock than surprise. I watched her scream on the computer when I broke the news via Skype, not the best way, perhaps, but given the distance—I live in Germany, she lives in Portugal—I had little choice.

All she could say was 'OK, so we're going,' and there was no more talk of travel until I showed up in Portugal, essentially to pick her up.

Maybe we'll talk about this during the trip, or maybe not. We'll have time to talk about so many things, at least I hope so! But at the same time, I feel quite daunted by and almost afraid of these kinds of conversations. It's so strange that the person you say you love the most in life, is also the person you're most afraid of talking about certain things with, and maybe worse, the person you know the least. I know much less about her life than the lives of certain friends, maybe even certain neighbors. All I really know is that she's my mother. Of course, I know other things about her, but that's the simplest answer: she's my mother. We tend to think that saying this says everything, when in fact being my mother is just one of the many parts that make her who she is.

We've never spoken much about ourselves, our lives, and dreams, and loves. . . . Maybe that's because we've always been more concerned with solving family and life problems—problems we could sense coming or that were already upon us—problems we knew about without anyone needing to speak of them, let alone spell them out. A simple exchanged glance or nod of the head was all it took, at most a single word.

I do know that my mum was not raised by her biological mother, but by a couple named Nho Armando O

Polícia and Nha Julia, in Santa Catarina, a small town in Santiago Island. Her biological mother gave her to this other family when she was two years old, and she has at least nine siblings from this adoptive family, uncles and aunties I have known since the day I was born. Auntie Mena, for example, is my godmother and she was one of the witnesses at my mother and father's wedding (indeed the same two people performed witness and godparent duties, though it's polite not to ask why!).

I also know that her childhood wasn't easy. I know from snippets of conversations and the occasional rant that she had to do a lot of work in the home and in the fields, planting, harvesting, and taking care of husbandry animals. Such chores are very common to anyone born in Cabo Verde.

She had childhood friends she talks about from time to time. She also often shares memories or tells stories she either heard or experienced herself. These anecdotes are amusing and she enjoys telling them, but I know there are others she avoids sharing, and I don't ask about them because I sense there is hurt there.

She says that one of her great regrets in life is that she was unable to attend school. Or rather she went, but not long enough to get through first grade. Household duties always took priority, and every day she'd be called home from class to do something or other. She knows her letters and numbers, but not how to combine them. I remember us as kids trying to teach her how to sign her name, but never managing it. We tried to apply the same methods we'd learned in school from our teachers, forgetting the major detail that she was our mother and not a kid, and that we were kids and not teachers. In a way, then, it's appropriate that the research I'll be conducting in Cabo Verde concerns educational programs in the revolutionary period.

She says she only saw her biological mother once, and for no more than thirty minutes. That was the day before she left for Portugal. When recalling that day, she says her mother must have been a great seamstress, especially of men's clothes, based on the items she saw hanging over the chair and spread across the table. My mum was twenty-one years old at the time. I also know she once sent her mother a package from Portugal, but got no reply.

She also only met her biological father once. Two men came to the house in Santa Catarina, riding a large horse. They told her to fetch her dad. She did so and her dad told her to go inside. She hid beside the window and heard a bit of their conversation. She remembers her dad pulling out a gun and yelling that the child was his now. The two men on the horse turned and left. When her dad came back inside, he told her that one of the men was her biological father. All she could think to say was that her dad might at least have let her meet the guy! She would have been around sixteen or seventeen years old.

Growing up in Portugal, I remember my mum working hard even during the summer holidays. But the word "holiday" in my house just meant a period of time when you didn't have to go to your first job, but you still had to do your second one. I remember her taking us with her because she had nowhere to leave us. She worked cleaning houses, cleaning buildings, cleaning stairways, from sunrise to sundown, and likely before and after besides. Of course, her work persona is not the only image I have of her. I used to love it when my Aunt Madalena came to visit, it was the only time I saw my mum cursing, joking, and fooling around. It was fun to watch the two of them: oh, so my mum uses swear words too!

She's not really had a holiday for the past thirty years. In fact, I don't recall seeing her spend more than one night away from home in all that time; home being the house she and my dad started building in Amadora in 1980 and that remains under construction today. She always insisted on returning home, even if it was getting late. Sleeping at other people's houses, even at her sisters', just wasn't for her.

I also remember, from when I was going through a phase of being fascinated by anything I could read, such as a love letter addressed to her. I lost track of the letter, old papers not being valued in a house under construction. Maybe I'll ask her about it during the trip. It was the first love letter I'd ever seen in my life.

She was married to my dad for twenty-five years (give or take). It came to an end one day, or one night, and I know she suffered a lot, but in silence. They have five daughters, but death took one away from her far too early in life. Then four years ago she had an accident and has been stuck at home ever since, taking care of her granddaughters, and waiting for the courts to resolve the insurance claim. She's never asked for anything in life besides good health and enough work to put food on the table and a roof over our heads.

She was the first person to encourage me to go to Cabo Verde, back when I was about to finish high school. She said that with my studies I could become a good teacher out there and be well paid. I just shrugged and said, "We'll see what happens, mama!"

She thinks she's only going to be in Cabo Verde for one month, or at least she claims to think so. But my plan (and somehow, I think she knows it) is for her to stay throughout the period of my stay—two and half months! We'll have to wait and see. What she's going to do with her time is up to her, although I have a fair idea. One of her mum's dying wishes was for Bia to seek out her biological mother!

Again, I guess we'll have to wait and see.

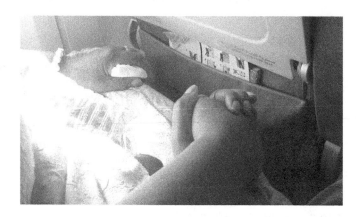

TWO

From Amadora to Praia

I spend a mad week rushing around Lisbon, having just spent a mad week rushing around Berlin trying to get my Cabo Verdean passport sorted out at the consulate. I could enter Cabo Verde with my Portuguese passport, but I didn't want to. I wanted to enter Cabo Verde for the first time using my Cabo Verdean passport, a political as well as an emotional act, essential to me. But such a goal did not prove easy to achieve. Even though the paperwork had been submitted months in advance, the consulate seemed simply incapable of issuing the passport on time. Why, an official at the consulate kept asking, was I going through so much hassle when I could simply use my Portuguese passport? I found the question extremely offensive. Had they no concept of what colonialism was? What it still is? What the liberation struggle was all about? Could they not see how saying such a thing revealed a lingering colonial mentality?

Livid about this, and the corresponding lack of urgency, I wrote an email to the head of the consulate. I explained my situation, expressed my disgust at their inability to comprehend why it was important for me to enter the country with my Cabo Verdean passport, and tried to convey why the trip was so significant, that it wasn't just a work trip but a homecoming for my mother. I got a very prompt and apologetic reply, with the assurance that my passport would be issued in time. A week later I had it in my hands, the potential emotion of the moment lost to plain relief.

Preparations for the trip are now just as manic in Lisbon. Nobody can quite believe that Bia is really going to Cabo Verde. It's like a dream come true not only for her, but for everybody: her neighbors and friends are as surprised, excited, and happy for her as she is. But perhaps the most poignant moment of the week, the image that stays with me as we head to the airport, comes when my father's eyes fill with tears when I tell him I'm not going to Cabo Verde on my own, that Bia is coming with me.

Like her, he has not been back to Cabo Verde since he left. It's just a shame I cannot afford to pay for both of them this time.

Check in is complete and we have our boarding passes in our hands. My sister has come to see us off: "See

you later," she says. We go through security and head to the gate.

My mum gets scared and a little bit confused by all the apparatuses on the plane. It's her first time flying and she's sixty-three years old. I try to explain things and put her at ease, especially because all the instructions are in Arabic. We hold hands during take-off and I talk to her constantly. She doesn't notice that we're already in the air, already flying. We've started our journey.

We stop off in Casablanca and wait around for four hours. Then we make an unscheduled stop in Gambia, wait around for another forty minutes and set off again. An hour and a half later we land in Praia. At precisely twelve hours and fifty-one minutes past two in the morning on July 26, 2013, my mother sets foot in Cabo Verde again after a gap of forty-two years.

THREE

Cabo Verde

They say nobody should go to Cabo Verde spiritually un-protected. I thought I was doing that, but then at the last minute, mum added two extra items to our luggage. The first was a small plastic bag containing some soil from our garden. Her neighbor told her that we should mix a bit of the soil into any kind of water we planned to drink in Cabo Verde, so as to protect our stomachs from the bacteria in the pipes.

The second was a bundle of three small plastic bags with a kind of dough inside. My mother says I'm to carry at least one of the bags with me wherever I go, that what's inside is not to be shared with anyone, and that it must be thrown away before we leave the country at the end of the trip. She will be drawn no further on the matter. But these are our first two steps for approaching Cabo Verde: drink water with dirt mixed into it; put a bag of dough in your backpack.

We are staying at my aunt and uncle's house in Vila Nova, a neighborhood in Praia's northern outskirts. I've only met this aunt once before, in Portugal. She's one of my mum's oldest sisters, and if I say 'one of' it's because I always get confused about who the oldest of the siblings is meant to be. In any case, she's a friendly, funny person, and she's so happy to have us visit that she's prepared us a lovely breakfast. Sadly, she lost her vision two years ago due to an illness, but she knows every corner of her house and every voice in the street.

So, our first day in Cabo Verde begins with this breakfast, nothing fancy, but all of it delicious: coffee, tea, milk, fried eggs, and homemade Cabo Verdean sausage, *longuiça d'terra* as we call it, along with bread and butter. I remember in Portugal, together with my grandmother and neighbors, cleaning and filling the animal intestines, to make the longuiça, and then putting them up to dry. Funny activities in summertime for a kid. The bread is traditional Portuguese bread, called *carcaça*, made from wheat flour and shaped into small loaves. There used to be more of a bread seam than actual filling, but it all depended on the bakery store where we got them.

I soon come to realize that although I've never been to Cabo Verde before, my entire childhood in Portugal was in many ways one long preparation for this day, our 'return' to the islands. That morning, the moment I pulled back the curtains at my aunt's house, it was like I'd been dropped back in Amadora, in a neighborhood like Santa Filomena, Damaia, 6 de Maio or Cova da Moura, or maybe all of them put together. The similarities are amazing. At first glance the place does not seem at all foreign to me. The houses are mostly unfinished and the street life and alleyways look very familiar, making me feel like I could probably find my way around without getting completely lost.

The atmosphere, the houses, the people, the sounds: it's as if I haven't left Amadora. Even the language, which might have been a big obstacle, is not. I find myself speaking Kriol from the moment I wake. I realize I'm going to have to dismantle the romantic, utopian image I had of Praia, an image based on the city my parents talked about. I doubt very much whether I'll see a *serenata* here like the ones my mother describes, performed by my uncle and his friends, wandering the streets of Santa Catarina on warm nights.

Even the Cabo Verdean music we used to listen to at home, indeed still listen to, helps to orientate me. By listening and singing along to the songs as kids, we not only improved our Kriol, we learned the names of places, traditions, struggles, stories; the different seasons in Cabo Verde, like the *azáguas*, the rainy season, which everybody is currently eagerly awaiting. That evening, walking around the neighborhood with my cousin, Ni, we pass a bar where people are excitedly gathering with their drinks, while techies prepare a stage with instruments and a sound system. We decide to go and investigate and I'm in for a wonderful surprise: Ferro Gaita, one of my favorite Cabo Verdean bands, are giving a free concert. It really is the perfect welcome!

To talk about Cabo Verde is also to talk about water, the biggest problem in the islands. We learn that the municipal supplier only turns the water on every other day: people must fill buckets, cisterns, and drums to cover for the next day, when the taps will run dry. There is no washing machine in the house, which means we must wash our clothes the traditional way, in plastic tubs or the old concrete washboard sink. But this is nothing new to me: it was the same in Portugal throughout my childhood. There is only cold water and no shower, so we have to bathe by pouring a mug of water over our heads, and for this we have no more than ten liters between us. Again, this is less a shock to the system than it is a step back in time. For this too was how it was at home in Amadora when I was young and the house often lacked all the modern conveniences we have now!

FOUR

Eugénio Lima

We go to the Eugénio Lima neighborhood and suddenly I'm out of my comfort zone, filled with trepidation. Not because the area feels unsafe, but because this is where my grandmother lives, as well as my grandfather on my father's side. I haven't seen or spoken to my grandmother for years, and I don't know the grandfather at all. We had a picture of him in our living room, but I've never met him, don't know the sound of his voice. I have heard stories about him, though. I know that he spent around ten years in São Tomé as a *contratado*,[1] working in the coffee and cocoa fields, known as *roças*. And I know that he worked in Portugal as a bricklayer, and that while he was there, he hid my father for two years. My father had been conscripted to go to Angola and fight on the Portuguese side, in what was known as the colonial war in Portugal and the liberation struggle in Africa, something he refused to do.

---

1. After 1869, when enslaved Africans, who had worked on the cocoa and coffee plantations, were formally freed as slavery was officially abolished by Portugal, the Portuguese colonial authorities began funneling contract laborers to São Tomé e Príncipe to fill labor shortages on the plantations, mostly owned by the Portuguese. These laborers were initially recruited in Angola and Mozambique, but after the Second World War, and following long periods of draught and famine in Cabo Verde, with scant support provided by the Portuguese government, many Cabo Verdeans were obliged to migrate to São Tomé e Príncipe and agree to exploitative labor contracts.

So, he asked for permission to go and see his father first, "For I may never see him again." The military granted him this request and he flew to Lisbon for the supposed last goodbye, and there he remained. He lived a kind of underground existence, working on construction sites, and hiding out in my grandfather's house.

We take a taxi to Eugénio Lima and ask the driver to drop us by the Mini Mercado Branco. Street names and numbers are not really used to get around out here, you're much better off using reference points, and in a way, this brings us closer to and makes us more familiar with the city. My uncle told us to get out at the market and ask around. I decide we'll ask for my grandfather's house first.

Neither grandparent knows we're in Cabo Verde, let alone that we we're visiting them today. It's not that we want to surprise them, more a simple precaution to minimize pre-travel stress, requests, and expectations. We start to ask after him in a barber's shop, where they tell us to ask the ladies in the hairdresser's shop. Then something remarkable happens: standing at the door of the hairdresser's, I ask if anyone knows him, referring to him by name, Manu; the first lady says no, but then a voice from the back of the shop yells out, "Are you Fernando's daughter?" Fernando is my father's nickname and how he's known to friends and family in Cabo Verde—his official name is José Borges and everyone calls him Borges in Portugal. "Yes, I am!" I reply.

I can't even see the woman's face, but she tells me my grandfather's house is right next door. I later learn from my grandmother that the lady is her sister, my great aunt Olivia.

And suddenly here we are, standing outside my grandfather's house, me looking in through the open door at a man in a chair who looks like an older version of my dad. Stupidly I ask: "Is this Manu's house?"

The old man says yes and beckons me in. I awkwardly proceed through the open door and introduce myself and my mother, as the old man offers me his hands.

Picturing a moment like this, we imagine lots of hugging and crying. But no such thing happens, it's quite a cold moment, nobody knows what to do. I look at him and he looks at me. We don't know how to treat each other; I don't even know whether to address him as Grandfather or Manu. So, we meet for the first time in an uncomfortable silence, slowly exchanging no more than cursory words.

Next stop is my grandmother's house. I approach an old lady in the street and ask for directions and she points me to a door where a girl is doing the laundry. I ask the girl if this is Vinda's house, and she confirms that it is.

I go inside and see my grandmother talking to another girl. She hasn't seen me and I ask the laundry girl not to say anything.

Then my grandmother turns around and bumps straight into me. She gives me a thorough looking over, trying to work out who I am. The moment she realizes, she says my name, hugs me, and starts to cry. I don't want to cry but I can't control my tears. I'm not crying simply from seeing her, there seems much more to it than that, though I couldn't exactly say what! My aunt Salomé now comes into the living room and says, "Don't cry." But she's crying too, and then I think I know why: my cousin Gilson recently died and nobody in the family here has yet had a chance to cry and mourn his passing in the company of others.

My mother comes in to join us and now she and my grandmother start to cry, for the same reason and doubtless many others besides.

The news of our arrival soon spreads and we find ourselves being paraded from door to door, proudly introduced to extended family members and neighbors. Everybody knows I'm family and they say I look like one of my aunts. In fact, I'm told this so many times by so many different people that I start to believe it must be true. But when I meet this aunt later on that day, I cannot see any resemblance at all!

We have lunch at my grandmother's and soon the tone changes and there are reprimands and even complaints: why didn't we send word? Why have we contacted them only now? Is it money issues? Trouble in the neighborhood? Death? The tenor and pace of the conversation pushes evermore in this direction and, though I've only just met them, I quickly tire of listening to their talk.

My mother and grandmother have some kind of private conversation. I only pick up a few words and phrases, but sense they are clearing the air. They haven't spoken for sixteen years and seem to be putting whatever happened behind them, sort of. It's at moments like these that I really admire my mother, her diplomacy, her patience, her strength, her courage to face up to things, to people, to feelings, to stories, all of this when so much harm has been done to her and her family.

FIVE

Pelourinho da Praia

On today's itinerary is a straightforward trip to the main market to buy fruit and vegetables, and other bits and bobs. The Mercado Municipal—or *Pelourinho* as it is called by the old generation—is in the Plateau in Praia's town center, and so I'm also looking forward to seeing the heart of the capital for the first time. But market day proves to be anything but straightforward.

We begin by walking around the market, checking prices, looking at types of fruit and fish and other things I've never seen in my life, my mother explaining things to me and telling me stories. I see a *caju* fruit for the first time and she points out where the nut (cashew, from *caju*) is located and describes how they are extracted.

I leave my mother with a cousin to bargain over buying some vegetables for my aunt, and go a little further into the market. I come to a halt before a stall where a lady is selling traditional Cabo Verdean medicine—*ramédi terra*. She encourages me to buy something, and we start chatting about what kind of medicines she has, what each one is, and what it's for. I don't want to buy anything, but she insists on showing me things, and I'm curious.

Then my mother arrives and joins in the conversation. Suddenly she asks the lady if she's from Monte Negro and if she knows somebody there named Angelina.

The lady says she's not from there, but tells my mother to go and speak to someone on the other side of the market, a woman named Bébé, who is from that region. We talk a little bit more about the medicines and, with a promise that I will come back and buy something before I return to Portugal, we head off to find Bébé.

I leave my mother to do the talking. She starts by asking the woman if she's from Monte Negro, a place she's never mentioned to me before, but that is apparently a village off the main road to Santiago. The lady says yes, she is, and my mother asks her if she knows anyone there called Angelina, though her real name is Paula Vaz. Again, the answer is yes, but she doesn't just know her, Angelina is her neighbor and sister-in-law or godmother, or perhaps both, it isn't quite clear. My mother then asks a third question: is this Angelina still alive or is she no longer with us? The woman now gives my mother a suspicious look and her eyes narrow as if to say, what kind of a question is that? My mum asks the same question again, without telling the lady who she is or why she wants to know. She just says that she needs to know, though she isn't sure what she'll do with the information yet. Undecided as to whether she should answer or not, the poor lady eventually says, "Yes, she's alive. Old, but very much living!"

There is a cold silence. The two women eye each other with a certain hostility. For what is probably only a matter of seconds, but feels like minutes, they say nothing, so I break the silence by turning to the lady and saying, "The reason she asks is because she's Angelina's daughter." The lady looks at me and then at my mother, she's clearly in shock. She closes her eyes and puts her hands on her head. I sense her struggling to register what she's just heard.

She looks at my mother again, not saying anything, just staring at her. Then she starts telling the story of Angelina's long-lost daughter, Bia. So, for all these years my mother has been a story! They knew she existed, but no one knew if she was dead or alive.

It's agreed that we simply must go there. The woman wants us to go right now, or failing that, the next day, but we say we can't, and suggest Thursday. We exchange numbers, take pictures, and make plans: on Thursday, August 1, my mother will meet her biological mother for only the second time in her life. I realize I'm not in any way prepared for this. We walk home in silence.

SIX

Assomada – Cutelo

My younger sister, who came to Cabo Verde last year and laid the groundwork for our visit, advised us on the best way of getting around the island—the Hiace. The Toyota Hiace is a type of minibus-van and they serve as the main form of public transport. They roam around Praia looking for people who need to get out to places in the countryside, or they patrol the road from Praia to Tarrafal, the main towns to the south and north of the island, picking people up and dropping people off. The drivers of these vans must compete for customers with rivals who run the same route—it's something of a battle to survive. Perhaps the most impressive thing is that, although this van can, by law, hold no more than twelve people, Hiace drivers routinely manage to squeeze twice that number in, and that's not counting the small children who are placed in strangers' laps.

When we arrive, the van to Tarrafal is empty. It will not depart until it has at least twelve passengers. We are the first to get in and we soon set off, but we're going nowhere, just driving around Praia, going up and down, back and forth, trying to fill up on passengers, a process that can easily take an hour. Nobody wants to get in an empty van because they know it means driving around for ages.

Most Hiace drivers are half-crazy, so you sit there with your heart in your mouth, saying your prayers, and crossing yourself whenever you pass a church. During our time in Cabo Verde, we will have numerous hairy experiences, including the driver who turned out to be drunk and drove insanely fast, barely bothering to brake on the blind bends of a mountain road. There was only me and my mother and two young men in the van. We all sat there frozen stiff, gripping onto the seat, looking at one another, expecting our lives to end at any moment. It got to the point where the two young men said, "Stop, stop right here," and they jumped out as fast as they could—they'd had enough. The driver carried on exactly as before, flying along with me and my mother in the back, shrieking with happiness or drunkenness, or a mixture of both. We could not get out, we had no choice, we were out in the mountains in the middle of nowhere in the dark, with no other way to get home.

But today our journey is not so bad. Our Hiace finally sets off for Tarrafal, though we're not going all the way. We're heading to Assomada/Santa Catarina, halfway between Praia and Tarrafal, right in the middle of the island, to see Luísa, my mother's childhood friend. I've known Luísa since I was little, from when she lived in Amadora, in Bairro Santa Filomena. She was the first person I told when I decided to bring my mother to Cabo Verde with me. It's a happy coincidence that she's in Cabo Verde visiting family at the same time as we are.

After a late breakfast at Luisa's, we walk into the town centre. We pass an old lady selling *azeti de purga*, an oil made from weeds and fruit seeds, that people say cures almost every kind of pain and skin disease.

Walking with my mother and Luísa is a journey of discovery, not the discovery of the town itself, but of my mother's childhood and youth. I learn about all the places she used to go, the neighbors she had, the street market, the indoor market, the church, the police station where my grandfather used to work, the military barracks next door, the communal places they went to cook bread or wash clothes. I could see memories unfolding through her facial expressions.

They stopped both at *Lavandaria*, the old communal washing place. They played around with the ladies washing their clothes, and even washed some pieces, remembering the old times, that as they said, "It was a hard time, but still left some saudade." She once shared the story of a Portuguese military who use to frequent the shop at their house. She used to do the laundry of one of them. One day he and others got called to join the colonial war in Guinea Bissau. He came to the house announcing that he was going to the front, saying, "Oh Isabel, I am going, but I am not sure I will return." And so it was, a few days after he land in Guinea, colleagues announced that he died at the combat front, two days after arriving.

My mum was born in 1950 and she proudly tells me that she herself took care of her birth certificate using the sparce information she managed to recover from the local church. She lived in Praia with her birth mother until 1952, when she was given away. But she remained in Praia, in the neighborhood of Achadinha, until 1958, when she was sent to live with her grandfather, Tubabu, in Jalalo Ramos. When she turned thirteen, she moved to Cutelo, in the province of Santa Catarina, and lived with Nho Armando and Nha Julia, until 1972, when the family moved together to Lisbon, during my grandfather's special and especial vacations from work, known as *férias graciosas*.

The house where she lived in Cutelo is still standing, though the area has changed: a new slaughterhouse has been built opposite it. Things start to get emotional. We stand across the street from the house she lived in from the age of twelve to twenty-one. She tells me that my grandfather sold it before they set off for Lisbon, but without telling anyone. All the family cried when they found out, but he'd made up his mind to go and the family had no choice but to follow. I look at the house and try to imagine how that conversation, or rather announcement, must have been.

The door is open and the new owner is at the door. We cross the street, my mother talking about the grocery store they used to have that was connected to the house. My mother introduces herself to the owner and they talk about the house for a while.

I know she wants to go in, but is too shy to ask. So, I ask the man and he says "but of course" and ushers us inside. "I live here," he says, "but in many ways the house is more yours than mine." He's being kind, but I sense he's also curious to find out more about the house and the people who once lived here.

His wife and daughter are inside, but the house is basically still the same and my mother walks around giving me a tour: the different bedrooms, the kitchen, the backyard, the terrace—and goddamn, it's quite emotionally heavy. When we're almost finished, my mum starts crying. At first, I think it's tears of joy, but then I see it's pain or some complicated mix of everything. She says, "If you only knew how hard I worked in this house!"

I decide it's best not to ask for any further explanation and I feel sorry for having caused all these memories to come to the surface. We say no more and the silence speaks for itself.

SEVEN

Monte Negro

Thursday, the day we arranged to go and meet Angelina, mum's mum, my grandmother, things don't get off to a great start. It turns out Bébé, the lady we meet at the market asked her niece (I think that was their relation) to accompany us. She has hired us a taxi, which proceeds to charge us the equivalent of thirty dollars, a small fortune out here. A Hiace would have been one dollar each.

We get the gossip in the end: the woman and the taxi driver are lovers, so it's a nice little scam they work. But also, she didn't want us to travel by Hiace, for matters of status—it's better to arrive by taxi. Whatever, island things I'll never understand.

The taxi drops us off in a small village, a smattering of perhaps a dozen houses gathered on either side of the road that leads to Santiago. A mountain looms over the village and I'm told you can see the sea from the top. But it's an isolated place. There's no piped water, no electricity, no telephone network. The village seems to be stuck in time. Perhaps the clock almost stopped forty-two years ago.

Everyone seems to have risen early in anticipation of our arrival. Children and adults sit in doorways watching us; news of our arrival has clearly spread fast. But even with all these people watching us, a strange silence fills the air, broken only by the occasional sound of some animal or a comment from one of the kids.

We are led to a house, and as we approach, I see there's a woman standing outside waiting for us. My mother embraces her firmly and asks if she's her mother. "No, I'm not your mother," the lady says, "I'm your sister, Francisca!" And they hug again and start to cry. Francisca was the only biological sister my mother ever met. When they were young, perhaps fifteen years old, Francisca spent a fortnight's holiday with my mother in Santa Catarina. Francisca was Angelina's second child and, like my mother, she was given to another family to raise. She later tells us that she suffered a lot with the family who raised her. She remembers returning after that fortnight with my mother and wanting to stay so badly she cried all the way home.

Francisca takes us inside. It's Angelina's house and the place is full of people, but Angelina is not home, so we wait. It turns out she's gone to a neighbor's house for help getting washed and dressed. After all, it's not every day that your first daughter comes to visit, and she wanted to look her best.

She arrives, a small, quiet, trembling old lady. My mother starts to cry, greets her by the door and hugs her tight. Angelina doesn't know what to do, she goes to hug my mother, but at the same time tries to push her away. I cannot even begin to imagine what's going on inside their heads.

My mother introduces me, telling Angelina that I'm her granddaughter. I do know to only give her a kiss on each cheek and a brief hug. It had been the same with my grandfather a few days earlier. But even with my grandfather I remember feeling more of a sense of warmth.

I register the moment, but afterwards I can't remember much about it. I recall my mother giving Angelina two towels and a kerchief, which I'd seen her preparing in Portugal. "If my mother is still alive, I'll give her this," she'd said.

I also remember everybody staring at me and my mother as if we weren't quite real, even saying as much. Some people even reached out to touch us, as if to confirm we were flesh and blood. It was a very strange situation for me. Then I remember going out for a walk around the village with the kids, taking pictures.

We have lunch at my aunt Francisca's house, where we're joined by two more sisters, Punota and Nelita. Nelita tells a funny story about being at a funeral and someone telling her that my mother had just turned up at her mother's house. She dropped everything and set off walking right away, something like six kilometers under a burning sun, anxious to meet a sister she only knew by name—Bia.

My aunts say that when Angelina found out Bia was in Cabo Verde and was coming to see her, people asked her if she'd cry. She replied with a very firm "No," and true enough she did not shed a tear. She was shaking, but she did not cry. Nevertheless, I can only imagine the weight of all those tears she held back inside.

EIGHT

Tchada Leitão – Jalalo Ramo

I've been charging around since the moment we arrived, visiting, seeking out and getting to know family, but also doing my research work on the PAIGC education programs developed during the liberation struggle in Guinea Bissau in the 1960s and '70s. This is the reason why I'm in Cabo Verde in the first place. It involves me doing research at the Amílcar Cabral Foundation and consulting their archives of the liberation struggle. Hopefully, through the foundation, I'll also gain access to former freedom fighters and get to interview them, especially those living in Santiago, as travelling to the other islands might be complicated.

But our next stop on the family trail is Tchada Leitão, to see my mother's sister, Bébé, and my mother's uncle, Pedrinho. We plan to also stop in Jalalo Ramos, tucked in somewhere amidst the mountains and valleys of Picos, to visit my mother's aunt, Belmira, my grandfather's sister. She helped raise my mother when Bia lived in Jalalo Ramos, from the age of six to twelve. We take a Hiace, which is once again completely packed and driven by a lunatic. We drove into the Picos also known as Achada Igreja, seat of São Salvador do Mundo municipality, and stop by Achada Leitão where some family members live. The landscape is totally dry and everybody is eagerly awaiting the rainy season—*azáguas!*—which appears to be running late.

In the fields we see people already preparing the land or replacing previously sown seeds that chickens and other birds have eaten. Kids are sent out into the fields after school to scare away the animals—*Panta Pardal, Panta Korbu* and *Galinha Matu*, as the song goes, *pa korbu ka tra sementi enteradu na terra*—so that they don't eat the seeds already planted, and in this way destroy a possible *colheita*—crops to harvest after the rainy season.

It is such a nice surprise to meet my aunty Bébé. She must be around seventy-five or seventy-six years old and she's one of the children my grandfather, Nho Armando, had outside his marriage. When she and my mother were young, she would claim, because an old man had told her, that my mother's real father worked at the Orgãos Market where he had a stall with two other men, Benício and Pachinho.

My mother asks her about this, but Bébé says she no longer remembers such things and changes the subject. The clear, if unstated, message is that what happened in the past should remain in the past.

The family essentially gets by on produce from the field and through selling the traditional baskets Bébé's husband and their daughter, Fatinha, make. But maybe there is some extra work they do that I'm unaware of.

In terms of my cousins, there is also Eli, who is twenty-two years old. She works at the house during the summer holidays, helping out another uncle while his wife is away. This set-up makes me really quite upset, because I saw the same thing happening with Nil, Eli's sister, who helps my aunt out during the holidays. It's like a labor maid system that operates inside the family, and I find it particularly uncomfortable to have my own cousins in a sense "serving" me.

Eli is not studying at the moment. She plans to go to Portugal, or to another country, to work and study there. But this is easier said than done because visas are very difficult to get, indeed leaving the country is generally not at all easy. This makes me even more upset for it reminds me how privileged I am, that having a Portuguese passport allows me to go almost wherever I want.

We go for a walk and take some pictures. We talk and it saddens me to learn how distant Eli is from the world, or rather how distant the world is from her. She asks me questions about my life in Portugal and she is astonished when I tell her I actually live in Germany. Alas, for many people in Cabo Verde, Portugal is still portrayed as the Promised Land!

In the afternoon we travel on to Jalalo Ramos, a locality situated near the hamlets Rão Fundo and Chão Formoso. We take another Hiace, which is not quite so packed this time, but the road is f****** terrifying! It is still made of loose stones, just as it would have been forty-two years ago, and it's wet and slippery because of a light rain that starts to fall. There is nothing that might pass for any kind of barrier between the road and the valley below. You really do need a strong hand and nerves of steel to drive around here.

My mother spoke a lot about this place, and the hardships of work during harvest time. Here very close to the top side of a mountain, the family owned a piece of land they called *tabuleiro*, a great place to plant the Feijão Pedra—Pedra beans.

She also used to tell us that harvest time was not a lucky time to harvest in terms of land and the produce. But it was the time for the luckiest ones to harvest some gold pieces, coins, and other belongings, buried by the dissident group, the *Rabelados,* meaning the Rebels. Formed in the 1940s, a part of the Cape Verdean society refused to follow the colonial rules of the Portuguese, in relation to the practice of Christianism, their refusal to speak the Portuguese language, and to follow colonial education. Persecuted because of their beliefs, they searched for refuge in the mountains of Tarrafal, Assomada-Santa Catarina, and Serra Malagueta, and built their own close community, that persists to this day, living in thatched houses and preserving the oldest customs and beliefs of Cabo Verde, following their own understanding of a Christian life.

Before they took refuge in the mountains, they buried all their material belongings in unmarked fields. According to the popular saying, from time to time, these same belongings resurface during the harvest season.

We have to walk the final two hundred meters to Pinhão, the location of the house, because the Hiace won't go any further. But we see there is someone waiting for us. This turns out to be Cesso, my mother's cousin. Who knows how old she must have been when my mother left? She leads us the rest of the way to the house, barefoot but with firm steps, for she is a shepherdess with a herd of cows for milking. When we get to the house, we find Aunt Belmira sitting in a corner. She is nearly ninety years old, but there's barely a wrinkle on her. She and my mother look at each other and then start to cry. It's a heavy sobbing and I don't really understand why, but am later told it's for two reasons: they haven't seen each other for such a long time, and also an uncle died some months earlier. It was the traditional mourning moment, crying for those who've passed away, and calling out to those on the other side to ask them to take care of this new soul and show it the right path.

After that, they sit down and talk as if a matter of days had passed rather than forty-two years. But they talk about old times and people who have died. I listen but soon get lost amongst so many names and memories.

They have a meal ready for us and urge us to sit down at the table. The food is served, but then they stand there and watch us. This is not the first time this has happened and it's really starting to get on my nerves—this business of serving us food but not sitting down to eat it with us. I'm beginning to feel like some kind of art installation. But I do have to understand that this is part of the culture.

As my friend Flávio later reminded me, "They have a meal ready for us and urge . . . it is a weird thing but for Cabo Verdean cosmology, embedded in famine psychology, it is demanded to give the food to the *hospriz* [the guest] even that you do not eat . . . the same applies in the case of sleeping: people give their bed and in some cases even sleep on the floor . . . it is a way to show hospitality, meaning 'the best that we have, we served to people that come to visit us (family members, close friends, or even strangers).'" Unconsciously, I too found myself also doing this at my own house.

Someone arrives and the heavy crying starts all over again. Afterwards my mother goes back into the living room and bumps into a childhood friend—Rosa. They are both overwhelmed with emotion to see each other.

The rest of the day is spent catching up with other childhood friends, beginning with Pedro and Paulo, twin brothers. She goes straight up to their house and asks for them. When they come to the door she just stands there and says, "How are you both?" Puzzled, they each answer "I'm fine," all the while staring at her. She asks them if they know who she is. They think about it, but they obviously don't. One of them says, "Well, your face looks kind of familiar, but I'm not sure from where." My mother says, "It's me, Bia d'Lulucha!" And you can almost see the memories rush into their heads. It's touching to see how surprised and happy they are to see my mother again.

They offer us food, which we accept, even though I've no more space in my tummy, and then they sit down and talk with such natural simplicity it's as if they're just picking up where they left off all those years ago. It makes me think about the complex effect time has on our ways of understanding and our feelings.

It has started to rain—praise the *azáguas*!—and there is no chance of a van passing by to pick us up. Even the Hiace drivers aren't crazy enough to tackle these roads now. So, we spend the night there. I get my own bed while my mother shares with her ninety-year-old aunt. They chat away as I drift off to sleep.

We return to Praia the next day. Everything is muddy and slippery after the rain. We have to walk back down to the road and a cousin gives my mum a stick for support. It starts raining again as we walk. The ride we get is in a pickup truck. There is no more room in the car, so my mum jumps into the back. I follow and that's how we travel back to the capital.

NINE

Tungiasis – Sand Flea

Purguinha or *pulguinha* is a small parasite that gets in between your toes and grows inside you. It would seem I've got one. The cure is to pull the parasite out and burn the wound with snuff, or *rapé*, tobacco-leaf dust that people normally inhale. My grandmother cannot live without her *rapé*.

When I ask Angelo, a construction worker who was doing some repairs at my auntie's house, for some rapé, he surprisedly asks me what I want it for. I tell him why and he laughs, "I thought *purguinhas* were out fashion," he says. They were evidently supposed to have been eradicated in Cabo Verde more than two decades ago. "Where in hell did you manage to find one of them?" he teases.

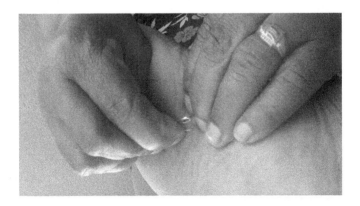

TEN

Gelo André

Today is the official welcome party for my mother, a family reunion in the village in Monte Negro that is also sometimes called Gelo André, from what I understand. My uncle Vital has organized it and invited everyone. All the various siblings are coming and most of the villagers too. People are even coming from other areas especially to join in with the festivities. Kitchens everywhere are a hive of activity. Some neighbors are peeling cassava, others plantain. Some people are getting fires started, ready to cook, others are setting up tables outside. Plates, glasses, and cutlery are brought out from every household. Kids and animals play or sit on doorsteps, giggling and teasing each other, waiting to be given another errand. My uncle brings out a petrol generator, so we will have electricity and music.

Angelina has stressed that she wishes to avoid having any deep conversations. She's eighty-six and I suppose digging up events from sixty-three years ago, when she had Bia, is not something she expected to have to do at her age. I get the impression she wishes to take the events of six decades ago with her to the grave.

All the same, my mother talks to her in a packed living room, plying her with questions. I'm running around playing with the kids, but my auntie takes me to one side and asks me to tell my mother that these kinds of conversations need more privacy. I come in to hear my mother asking Angelina who her father is. Angelina is reluctant to say, and asks my mother why she needs to know? The room is full of children, and a number of adults are following the conversation. The only solution I can think of is to ask everyone to leave the room. I leave too, though not before placing my dictaphone on the table. I imagine the conversation getting emotional and my mother forgetting some piece of key information afterwards.

ELEVEN

Childhood memories

The old washboard sink. It brings back happy memories of childhood and summer holidays. I remember washing clothes in one at home with my mother and grandmother. Made of concrete, they were almost impossible to move from one place to another. The prototype washing machine, built to last a lifetime. In hot summers, after everything was washed and hung up on a rope to dry, we'd be treated to the famous *banho de mangueira*—hosepipe shower. We were always hot, sweaty, and dirty from playing in the garden, the backyard, or the dirty road that was our street's playground. Or we'd come back covered in bits of corn, peas, or bean sprouts after messing around in the vegetable patch. Sometimes we were put inside the washboard sink and given a good scrubbing.

Here in Cabo Verde, at my aunt's house and many of the surrounding houses, we wash our clothes in an improvised sink using plastic tubs and a wooden scrubbing board. But my trip down memory lane cannot be complete with a *banho de mangueira*, water rationing won't allow it. I'll have to wait for a *banho de chuva*, a rain shower, instead.

TWELVE

Cidade Velha

Cidade Velha, "Old City," previously called *Ribeira Grande* "Large River," is said to be one of the oldest European settlements in Africa, although it ought really to be called an occupation. It is located in the south of Santiago Island in the valley of Ribeira Grande, one of the oldest European occupations and colonial towns in the sub-Saharan tropics. The town features some of the original street layout. Rua de Banana, Banana Street, the oldest street in this oldest occupation, is something of a marker in terms of the history of colonialism and slavery, but there is nothing written about it on any of the information boards dotted around the village. Two churches, a royal fortress, and the Pillory Square still remain. The city simply "is" a Portuguese settlement in Cabo Verde, albeit one rescued from ruin by funding received from "a Spanish institute," according to the information placards displayed beside the tourist center. Then again, the people who rebuilt it in 2005 were the free descendants of the enslaved Black people who were forced to build it in the first place.

But it's a nice place to be, located in the middle of an enormous valley currently connected to the sea by a dried-up river. Hopefully the *azáguas* will fall in sufficient volume this year to refill it.

Right in the middle of town, in the center of the main square, is the most emblematic and somber monument in Cidade Velha—the *pelourinho*. A marble pillar dated from the sixteenth century on the center of Pillory Square, surrounded by a small staircase leading up to it, was where enslaved people were sold, punished, and beaten to death.

In the same square, African men now sell handicrafts, and tourists walk around taking pictures. I am amazed to see people posing for photos here. I see a young Black woman carrying a baby ask her partner to take a photo of her. She climbs the steps, the baby strapped to her front, turns to her partner and smiles. Click. Then she raises her hands up as if she were shackled to the stone. "Look," she says, loud and clear, "now I look like Escrava Isaura!"She gives a big laugh and, click, another holiday snap for the album.

I'm appalled by this image and all the ignorance it implies. I too watched the "Isaura: Slave" a Brazilian telenovela on TV that tells the story of the struggles of Isaura, a mixed-race slave in the nineteenth century. It was a hit in Portugal, and broadcast several times since its production in 1977. I'm still stunned to witness the poisonous effect such an uncritical romanticizing of historical events can have.

I take some flowers from a nearby garden and place them on the *pelourinho*, for it is, of course, also an unmarked grave. I tell whatever spirits are around to rest in peace, or maybe not to rest but to keep on rocking the world, in a way to *bulimundo*—a Kriol expression, as well as a male first name, meaning *bulir o mundo*—to "agitate" the world—as we say.

As we climb the hilly road up to the fort that overlooks the old city, my mother is bitten by what had looked to be a harmless dog taking a nap in the sun. We had to go to a nearby health care center. There is no taxi around and it's too far to walk, but a car passes by and people flag it down and ask the driver to take us. He agrees and we get there in good time. However, my mother is really upset when the nurse says she has to have an anti-rabies injection.

THIRTEEN

Tarrafal

The last time my mum spent a night in a hotel, or at least in a hostel, was October 2, 1972, after sailing into Lisbon on the *Manuel Freire* ferry. She says it was a seven-day voyage from Cabo Verde, *seven dias Riba d'agu mar ta anda.* The big boat docked on the Rio Tejo and a small boat took them to shore and the Lisbon Custom's House. She spent her first night in Lisbon in a hostel in Caís do Sodré, and the next few nights in a nun's convent. She was twenty-two years old. The nuns found her a job as an in-house maid for a Portuguese family, so she moved in with them. Apparently, it was common for the nuns to act as intermediaries between new arrivals from Africa and households seeking domestic workers.

We are going to spend a night in a hotel in Tarrafal, on the other side of Santiago Island, at the northernmost point. On a clear day they say you can see over to the volcano on Fogo Island. I really want to climb to the top of that volcano one day, but we shall see!

As per usual, we take a Hiace. It's supposed to go directly to Tarrafal, but when we get to Santa Catarina we're made to change to another van. We then spend over an hour driving around searching for passengers to fill it up. It's Saturday, market day, so the streets are packed with people buying and selling things, or just browsing and walking about. We drive around the market and then stop on a corner, then drive around the market again. After completing several such circuits my mother decides she wants to buy guava. She's seen it several times now and says it looks good. We tell the driver to stop, but he and his conductor-friend don't want us to get out because they're afraid we won't come back again. The conductor offers to go for us. I give him some money and he comes back with $200 (escudos) worth of guava. It's all rather convoluted and stressful, but I find I'm starting to like the Hiace system and the way everyone is, for the most part, so cool about things.

That said, by the time the van is finally full, everyone inside is pretty fed up with driving around listening to the driver shout—louder and louder—*Tarrrafallll, Tarrrafalll, Tarrrafalllll, directo!*

The fields here are still green, having got more than their fill of water from Hurricane Humberto. Farmers and farmhands, and everyone else besides, are in the fields re-weeding—*ramonda*. Everyone has to help with this, young and old, like it or not. Subsistence farming is still a major source of food and income for the country and, given intermittent droughts, the land must be properly cared for. Amílcar Cabral was so aware of this that he studied agronomy in parallel to his becoming a revolutionary leader, for he knew that the future of the territory would be dependent on agricultural development.

Santa Catarina mountains also tell us other stories of Cabo Verdean rebellion and resistance. It was here that the first *quilombo*, a marron society in the archipelago—Quilombo of Djulange, was created in the eighteenth century under the leadership of Domingos Lopes. Even after his capture and public execution, Djulange continues to exist as a space of resistance and freedom. Its story still waits to be written, as it is remembered from the oral history passed from generation to generation.

We eventually reach Tarrafal, a small and quiet little town. We are staying at Pension Mille Nuits. We pay up-front, leave our things in the room (whose bed sheets are stamped with the logo name St. Joseph Hospital – Fatima Unit 1971–1972) and go for a walk around. We don't even have a map with us, but I'm pleased to see my mum is not afraid of a bit of adventure.

We find the beach just as the fishermen are coming in with the day's catch, so fresh a lot of the fish are still alive. Everybody gathers around the boats to buy or just to look.

Two friends of mine, Nuno and Jacira, along with their kids, Zion and Malik, come to join us for the day. We have a very relaxing time, doing nothing, chatting, lazing around in the white and warm sand, and playing with the kids in the water.

After they leave, we head back to the hotel, albeit for no good reason—five minutes later we're back out again looking for a place to eat. In the end we decide to buy takeaway grilled chicken and eat it in the park in front of the church. It gets a little bit crazy when the local dogs start to circle, surrounding us in the hope of a bone. "Poor mama," I say, "forced to share chicken bones with a pack of dogs because her daughter can't afford to take her to a restaurant!" She smiles.

The next day, we have breakfast and then go out for another walk. Tarrafal is really quiet and there doesn't appear to be a great deal to do. By nine o'clock we're back on the beach where the water is warm, despite it having rained. While walking around we came across a street called Rua Cidade de Amadora, which causes us a good deal of amusement. It seems there's no escaping our hometown!

It turns out that Amadora and Tarrafal are sister cities. This seems incongruous: Amadora is landlocked, without even a river passing through it, while Tarrafal sits at the northernmost tip of Santiago Island, its entire being focused on the sea. What do these two distant places have in common? The question is not easily answered, perhaps only the official documents signed between the two municipalities can tell us. But in the absence of such information, we dare to speculate.

Tarrafal is synonymous with the concentration camp located at its border, in the village of Chão Bom. Established in 1936 by the Portuguese Estado Novo, it was officially called the Cabo Verde Penal Colony, but became known as the "Slow Death Camp." Political prisoners and social subversives, initially from Portugal, later from the colonised African territories, were sent there to waste away. The prison remained open until May 1, 1974, when it was closed as a consequence of the Carnation Revolution of April 25, 1974. In 2009, the site was transformed into the Museum of Resistance.

It was in their almost inaccessible mountains that the Rabelados found refuge from the Portuguese persecution. It sometimes ended with the imprisonment of some of their members in the concentration camp, for their resistant act against colonialism.

Cut off from the rest of Greater Lisbon, some parts of Amadora can also feel like a prison. The same year that the Tarrafal camp was turned into a museum, the various neighborhoods of Amadora became officially designated as "sensitive urban areas," giving the police special powers to carry out raids and surveillance. The Portuguese government was, in other words, making an implicit connection between immigrant and ethnic spaces, and criminality.

But just as most of the prisoners in Tarrafal were subversives rather than criminals, so too has Amadora developed its sense of resistance and political consciousness. Collectives began to form, encouraging citizens to celebrate their culture and take a stand: the theater group Undi ki da Ki Panha, the youth organizations like Associação Encontros, Plataforma Gueto, Associação Cavaleiros de São Brás, Associação Moinho da Juventude— one way or another, all these groups remain true to the spirit of what the prisoners in Tarrafal were fighting for, and continue the anticolonial, anticapitalist struggle.[2]

Our plan for the day, or more accurately my plan for the day, was to stop off at Serra Malagueta on the way back to Praia from Tarrafal. But it proves to be the typically overambitious plan of someone who hasn't a clue about the island and its weather moods. The Serra Malagueta has a mountain microclimate anyway, but given the recent rain, it would barely be possible to lay one firm foot in front of another. When clouds cover the mountain top, old people say, *Monti dja marra cabeça!*—the mountain has put its hat on!

---

2. Recently, two other social movement were created in the city. They are the activist group Movimento Vida Justa, and the community-based meeting space Mbonji67.

There are stories of landslides and rockfalls making the road there impassable, and of sudden thick fogs. To drive into the mountains in these conditions someone would have to walk along in front of the car with a torch making sure it's safe to continue. And if it's not, you better hope some friendly local offers you a bed for the night. I guess Serra Malagueta will have to wait for another time.

We go to the Tarrafal concentration camp museum instead. My mother used to tell us stories about the place, stories her father told her back when they lived nearby. As a policeman, he knew a thing or two about what went on behind those walls. One story stuck in my head about a room in the camp they called the *frigideira*—frying pan. I found the name cute, but the story frightening when I first heard about it as a kid. All these years later, I realize it was a solitary confinement chamber with no ceiling, used to punish prisoners who stepped out of line.

We finish our trip at Ribeira Prata, another beach, but one where there are giant black rocks instead of sand. But my mum is clearly tired, so we hop aboard the next Hiace and head back to Praia. There, in total contrast to the top of the island, a hot night awaits us.

FOURTEEN

Newspaper – Jornal Voz di Povo

When I was a child in Portugal, a package would come from Cabo Verde to our house every two or three months. It was no more than a bundle of white pages wrapped in brown paper with our address scribbled on the front. But whenever the postman delivered it, I couldn't wait for my dad to get home and open it.

My uncle used to send old copies of the *Voz di Povo* to my father and, albeit with a two- or three-month delay, we were thus able to keep up with events in Cabo Verde. This would have been my first exposure to written news from Cabo Verde, as opposed to the word-of-mouth news we got from friends and neighbors, as well as written Kriol.

Most exciting of all, in 1992, *Voz di Povo* started to publish a youth supplement. I remember my dad opening the package and then flipping through the newspapers to find it for me. I used to treasure these supplements and save them reverentially in a plastic bag, re-reading them from time to time. But in a house that was under constant construction, things forever being moved around and the bag got lost in some clear-out or other.

I decide to go to the national library in Praia and seek out this little slice of my childhood memory. I find the newspaper and supplement, but have no idea what months or years I'm looking for. Then suddenly I come across some familiar pages and I'm overwhelmed with nostalgia. It makes for a very happy day.

FIFTEEN

Quintal do Burro

As a child, Cabo Verde was a place I had to invent for my-self, my imagination feeding off names: Além Katchor, Ponta d'águ, Tira Chapéu, Fazenda, and so on; names from stories or that I picked up from adult conversations. I imagined Ponta d'Agu as a place full of water, even with a waterfall; Além Katchor would be full of dogs; Fazenda a big green farm. To my disappointment, Ponta d'Águ is a very dry place, there are almost no dogs in Além Katchor, and Fazenda is just a road today.

And then there was Quintal do Burro, a green space in the middle of the big city. One day in Praia, when we're on our way home, my mother looks up and says, "Quintal do Burro used to be around here." I suggest we go take a look. Quintal do Burro was another one of those mythic names, a place she used to talk about as being a vast field of sugar cane, tamarind, and palm trees beside a big well.

My mum used to live in Achadinha, whether before or after Santa Catarina I'm not sure, and whenever they had to go to Plateau to take my grandfather his lunch at the barracks (Quartel Jaime Mota), they had to cross Quintal do Burro. She'd always assumed the place didn't exist anymore, but as we walk in its direction we stop and ask some people if the well is still there. They tell us it is and when we get there, I see my mum's face fill up with memories. The place is quiet and peaceful, and it's refreshing and inspiring to see my mother rediscovering a place like this again.

She stops and stands by the well and looks down at it without saying anything. Eventually she mutters, "I always thought it was much bigger than that, but I suppose it's still the same size." She steps back and carries on staring at it, and I wonder about what kind of images must be passing through her mind.

SIXTEEN

João Teves

Armed with the information my mother wheedled out of her mother, we set off for Orgãos. She has family there and the plan is to ask them if they knew someone called Ivo who used to work at the market. It's my mother's decision to go, I simply follow. I really don't want to pressure her to do anything.

Unfortunately, nobody there knows of or remembers him. Mum seems to give up on her quest—"There is nothing more I can do!"

I'm not so sure. When we get back to the house, I decide to give it one last shot and listen to the recording of the conversation my mother had with her mother. I haven't listened to it before and the sound quality is not very good. I play it back two or three times trying to pick out some piece of overlooked information.

And actually, there is some: João Teves is mentioned. João Teves is a locality in Orgãos, where my mother's biological father, Ivo, used to live. The next day I decide to go back to the main market. If we managed to track down my mother's mother just by asking around at the market, maybe we can find her father that way too. But I decide to go on my own. I tell my mother I'm going to the Amílcar Cabral Foundation.

I do go there. The Amílcar Cabral Foundation is where I've been conducting most of my research and holding interviews. They have given me use of one of the computers to access the Internet, print files, and scan documents. I finish a bit of admin, then head for the market.

My method is basically the same as my mother's. I take a deep breath to gain courage and then go over to a random woman and ask her if she's from João Teves. She says she's not, but a woman over there is. I go over and ask this other woman, then give her all the information I've got: that I'm looking for a man named Ivo who worked at the market, is believed to be from João Teves, and had an estranged daughter. The woman replies, in front of a crowd of curious onlookers, that there are only two men in the region called Ivo, and one of them passed away fifteen years ago. But she doubts he's the man I'm looking for as she was his neighbor, and she never heard of him having another child.

Then she addresses me in really aggressive Kriol, saying "What do you want to go bothering him for anyway, he's already passed away?" I keep my cool and very quietly say that the man is my grandfather. Even angrier now, she asks me where I got this information. Again, I stay calm and say that it was from my grandmother, that she told me this just a few weeks ago.

Now the lady takes pity on me, as does everyone around listening in. "Oh, poor little thing," she says, "coming from so far away to look for her family in the market of all places, what a sad story."

Then she asks about my mother, did she never talk to me about her father. I say that my mother never met her father and he never met her. The pity for me grows.

The woman says she lives next door to Ivo's daughter, and I beg her to simply tell her neighbor what I've just told her. I say I'll come back the next day, that I merely wish to know if we're talking about the same Ivo.

She agrees to this and I head home worrying about how to present this information to my mother. I get home and wait for the "right" moment, then try to look casual as I fill her in on my day, as per usual. But I'm shaking as I speak and my words are met with silence. However, if I've learnt anything in Cabo Verde it's that silence can be expressive.

SEVENTEEN

Praying mantis

It was the last of my savings. I always knew that after splurging on this trip, if I didn't get a scholarship, I'd have to find another way to finance my studies in Berlin. All the same, I decided it was worth the risk because later on, with a job, such a long trip would be impossible. I came to Cabo Verde with a very clear work goal, to research PAIGC education policy during the Liberation War, and I'm managing to do it. In fact, I find my formal research—academic and mapped out—and my informal research—personal and free-flowing—feed off each other, the one complementing or inspiring the other.

I get two big pieces of news today. I've won a Rosa Luxemburg scholarship and will therefore be able to fund my PhD! I'm at the Amílcar Cabral Foundation when I see the email. I'm too afraid to open it at first, because a big fat No is almost guaranteed in such circumstances. But then I open it and my God, I don't think I've ever read and understood German so fast in my life! I leave the foundation and run screaming to my mother, who I've left sitting at Cruz Grande, enjoying the view of the sea. Everybody stares at me as I run over yelling *Ganhei, Ganhei*, I won the scholarship! My mother says I looked like a *"baca parida,"* a cow giving birth, which I assume is some kind of Cabo Verdean expression. It's not a great look, but I don't care, I've got the economic means to carry on my studies and rescue the PAIGC education program from oblivion.

Still glowing with this great bit of news, we head to the market, where we get the second piece of good news: it's the same Ivo; we've found my mother's family on her biological father's side.

The lady is impatiently waiting for me when I get there. The moment she sees me, she screams, "I've been waiting for you all morning, your aunt just called me wanting to know if you'd shown up yet." At which point she notices my mother standing next to me. "Is this your mother? You didn't tell me she was here!" But there's no time to answer, she grabs my hand and says, "Come on, your uncle is over there waiting for you."

Me and my mother follow this woman, who has the sense of purpose of an army. She introduces us to a man and says, in a loud voice, 'Here is your niece, and this is your sister.' Everyone is watching us, and we're all simply paralyzed. The only thing we can think to do is say "Hi" and greet one another. While we stand around in awkward silence, the lady calls my aunt and says, "Augusta, she's here, your niece and your sister are here standing with your brother Zé Carlos." Then without further ado, she heads off to take charge of her market stall again.

The three of us remain where we are, frozen, looking back and forth at each other. My newfound uncle eventually breaks the impasse by saying, "Well, let's go to Fazenda, my other brother works there."

We go there in a red pick-up truck. My mother sits in the front seat and I pile in the back. Then he parks the truck in front of a shop next to the stop where I get the bus in to the Plateau every day. My other new uncle apparently works here.

We go into a shop and Zé Carlos says, "Here they are!" We all go outside and again, all we do is stare at each other. After several silent minutes, my uncle says the only thing he has to offer is some fruit juice. We go back into the shop and I have a juice and my mother says maybe she'll have one too. We stand to one side while my uncle, António, remains in the corner. He looks very thoughtful with his arms crossed.

I tell him to come and stand beside us, "There's no need to be scared!"

"I'm not scared," he says, "just shocked. I never thought this day would come."

They are still in complete shock over seeing my mother. She's in shock too, of course. But they were expecting to meet a niece, not a sister.

It's arranged for us to go to my grandfather's house the next day. By the sounds of things, my aunt Augusta is eager to meet us.

In Portugal we call them *Louva-Deus* [praying mantis]. I was afraid of them as a kid because adults said not to play with or stare at them, else they might eat your eyes. But in Cabo Verde they call them *Saúde*, meaning "health." It's said they bring luck and are a sign of good news. I learned this only a few days ago and it must be true because there was one on my bed when I woke up yesterday. And hopefully my luck will continue, because I found another one in my room this morning.

EIGHTEEN

Lage

My mother and I didn't say a word all day about what had happened at the market, or about the last few days and how she was feeling about it. On the one hand, I'd really like to know what her feelings are, but on the other, I'm reluctant to ask. I want her to take her time, without me putting any pressure on her. Feelings need time to find their means of expression. They have to find their own words. Over the years I've learned not to ask too many questions, but to read the environment, the mood, the way my mother moves, or expresses herself through her eyes. I've learned that people don't necessarily need to put their feelings into words, they can express things in other ways. Or so I like to tell myself.

I had a very strange vision this morning. I'd just woken up and opened my eyes and the first thing I saw were two light white balls moving around above my mother, who was still asleep. They were just hovering over her, but also opening and closing, and whenever they opened, they let out a white light, and then they closed again.

I closed my eyes and rubbed then, not really believing what I was seeing, assuming it was some kind of optical illusion because my brain was still half-asleep. But when I opened them again, I saw the same thing. I watched the two lights for a while, wondering what on earth they were.

Then I closed my eyes for a moment, and when I opened them again, the lights were gone.

I remained quiet and I didn't say anything about it to my mother when she woke up.

My uncle will pick us up at seven, so we're up early to get ready. We travel in the red pick-up truck again. My mother goes in the front with my uncle and his wife, and I sit in the back with my uncle's daughter.

We pass Orgãos and follow the road to Assomada. We pass Rui Vaz and the yellow iron bridge, and then a little bit further on, we pull over at the end of a stone pathway where there is a sign saying Centro de Artesanato. We get out of the car and my uncle tells us to follow the path, they have to go to church for some ceremony.

We wait and look around for a moment, then set off up the path. A tall lady comes the other way, all dressed in black, her eyes full of tears. When she reaches us, she embraces my mother and proceeds to cry and cry. My mother tries to comfort and calm her, "Don't cry, there's no need to cry, no one's to blame."

Then the woman looks at me and does the same thing, embraces me and cries. She turns to my mother and says, "I'm not crying just because you're here, I'm crying because of my dad who was always waiting for this moment and told me before he died that the only thing preventing him from dying in peace was that he had a daughter he could not register in his name or show the same love he'd shown his other children."

She grabs my mother by the hand and leads her up to the house. She's my aunt Augusta, it turns out. Inside the house are my cousins and Augusta's husband, who is also in a flood of tears.

We spend the next hour listening to family stories, especially the story of how the woman from the market told them about me. Augusta says she didn't believe it at first, but then she couldn't sleep at night and she kept asking her husband if it could really be true. She says the only thing she said to the saint she has in her room was, "If you've already sent us our niece, then please send our sister to us too."

We have breakfast, buying fish from a lady who passes by, and cooking it together. My uncles, António and Zé Carlos, come to join us and we spend the afternoon talking about our lives, learning about the plants in the garden and the animals around the house. We talk about Ivo, how the house used to be when it was his, the house they all grew up in, and what's changed now that Augusta lives there with her family. We also talk on the phone to another sister who lives in France and whose name is Fátima.

They are really lovely people, straightforward and kind-hearted. They tell us that my grandfather went off in search of my mother three times. The first time in Jalalo Ramos, when my mother was about four or five years old. Afraid of what the family's reaction might be, he did not say he was the girl's father but rather an uncle, saying he came as an uncle to see the child and on behalf of the father who would also like to come and see her and perhaps register the girl under his name. He asked for a glass of water and a child was sent to get one. He always said that as soon as he saw the girl come in barefooted and hand him the glass, he knew it was his daughter. He could tell just by her fingers. Alas, the family taking care of my mother at the time wouldn't let him take her.

He went back to Jalalo Ramos at a later date, but my mother was no longer living there. The third time he went looking for her was in Santa Catarina, but he was told she no longer lived in Cabo Verde, the family that had adopted her had taken her to another country where she was to become a nun.

My auntie says she sometimes asked him why he didn't keep searching. He didn't like to talk about it and could answer testily: "Search where? I don't even know her name. I wouldn't know where to even start. Don't bother me about this again!"

It seems that after having my mother, my grandmother vanished inside Cabo Verde. According to the other side of the family, she never went to Orgãos again, not even for the death of her brother. Why, nobody knows.

Augusta says that one day her father heard that one of his nephews had become a father, but didn't want to register the child. My grandfather called him up right away and said, "Look at me, I've got a daughter I've never even met, a child I couldn't give my name to. Every child has the right to take their father's name. You've got the opportunity to do it, so do it, don't be stupid!"

Before we leave it's arranged that in two days' time we will return for an official family gathering.

NINETEEN

Retelling the story

Maggi: Diana, is your mother at home?

Diana: Yes. She's resting in her room

(Maggi enters the house and goes into the room.)

Maggi: *Tia*, wake up! Did uncle Ivo use to work as a door-man at the Orgãos market alongside Benicio?

Augusta: Yes!

Maggi: How many kids did uncle Ivo have?

Augusta: What kind of question is that?

Maggi: Did uncle Ivo ever tell you about another child of his, say that it's not just you four?

Augusta: Yes!

Maggi: *Mudjer labanta!* Get up, woman, because your niece was in the market today asking after your family!

Augusta: *Kusé!?* What!!?

(She jumps out of bed, trembling.)

Augusta: Did you ask her name?

Maggi: No!

Augusta: Did you get her phone number?

Maggi: No!

(Augusta looks at her angrily.)

Maggi: I didn't think of anything like that. How do you expect me to think to ask all these things? She just showed up and started to ask me all these questions, *e panhâ-m di surpréza*, she took me by surprise!

Augusta: (looking her in the eyes) Maggi, if I don't hear from this girl again it will be your fault!

Maggi: Noooo! Don't say that! She'll come. She's the one who's interested. And I told her to come to the market tomorrow and meet me in the same place. I was so surprised that I didn't even remember Zé was at the market too. But she'll come back, I know she will. When she left, she asked the Virgin Mary to help her find her family!

(Me listening to this story with a big smile, not remembering saying this last bit.)

Maggi: *Tia*, the moment she turned and started to walk away, I knew she was from your family. *Minina*, girl, she is as big as you, her back is just like yours, she has a big ass just like you do, she walks like you do . . .

Augusta: God Maggi, and you didn't even think to ask her name? What if she doesn't come back?

(This is how I recall Maggi at the family gathering, retelling the story of when she got home from the market that day.)

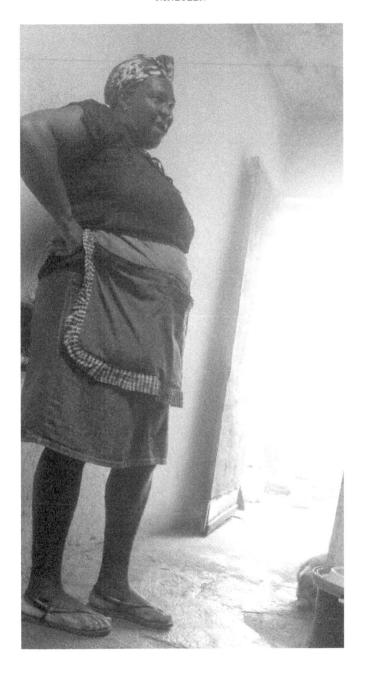

TWENTY

Fonte de Almeida

My grandmother wants to show me where my father was born. She says it's important I see the place because it's *Biku di bu pai sta nterádu*, where my father's "beak" is buried, the beak being the placenta. The place is called Fonte de Almeida. Some of my uncles and aunties are there working in a field, doing the first *monda*. I want to help them, but they are quick to discourage me. They say I don't know how to do such work, to which I reply that I do. "Please don't treat me like some city princess from Portugal," I say, "because I am most certainly not that!" And with this I simply start doing the same as them.

In Portugal we used to have a vegetable patch at the back of our house and I remember doing this kind of work, weeding, turning the soil, planting seeds, watering, weeding again; and then harvesting, picking the corn, the tomatoes, the runner beans and broad beans, the peas, the lettuces, and so on; and then helping the neighbors with theirs, spending the entire summer picking and peeling our harvests.

After a while, my grandmother says we must go, and I just follow. The soil is soaking wet and it's very difficult to walk on in flip-flops. I take them off and walk barefoot. She leads me to a ruin of a stone house. It's covered in overgrown plants, it's impossible to make anything out at all. But she wants me to know the story of the place, where a house used to stand proud and where my father was born. She points to a particular corner and says it used to be a room with a bed, and that under that bed they buried the placenta after he'd been born. She tells me about the neighbors they used to have and what life was like back then, the jobs my father did as a boy, working *nos paralelos*, paving the stone road we now walk on.

Next up she takes me to meet a group of old folks who've all known my father since the day he was born. One of them is Nha Ofémea, the woman who delivered him. She's ninety-seven years old, but she doesn't look it with her kind smile and her white head scarf. I meet her husband too, Nho João Pereira, and we all talk for a while, until a car comes to pick us up, along with some of those who've been laboring in the field. Nha Ofémea gives me her blessings and we leave.

I'd expected my grandmother to pay for the taxi ride, but no. She says she hasn't any money, not even the 100$00 we need to complete the 400$00 fare. I only have 300$00 in small notes and the driver can't change my 1000$00 bill. In the end he lets us off the extra 100$00. We get out and I shake my head, I guess some things will never change with my grandmother.

TWENTY-ONE

Her body and my scars

I have this beautiful picture of my mother in my photo album. I took it when she was in the kitchen one day, preparing the traditional Cabo Verdean breakfast of *cuscus*. We had cuscus for breakfast every Sunday morning throughout my childhood. We ate it with milk, butter or sugar, or just plain, or sometimes dried in the sun and sprinkled with cinnamon, like popcorn.

She smiles into the camera and the light from the windows falls straight on her face. In another picture she's utterly absorbed in her cooking, but in this one she's smiling. I remember I was looking at her and noticed how beautiful she looked and, realizing I had my camera in my hand, I said, "Mama, turn around," and she turned and smiled and "click," I took the photo. It was an old camera so I had to wait for it to be developed to see how it turned out.

I used to like looking at pictures of my mother when she was young. I loved her big afro hair, her elegant, Black-Power style, how cool she looked, how cool my dad looked. I was mesmerized by the strength of those images and the power and dignity they conveyed, so far removed from the clichéd image of the suffering African immigrant in Portugal. So, Angela Davis' afro was not the first image of Black Power I saw. My mother's afro was. My dad's afro was. My aunties' afros were, and the covers of the African vinyls we had in the house were too. That was Black Power, before I even knew such a thing existed. But I could see it, in photos of weddings and christenings— that photo album was my first lesson in Black Power. In these photos they didn't look like my parents, but like film stars. I used to try and imagine, and I still do sometimes, how their lives must have been back then. What did they do, where did they go, how did they meet? Sometimes I asked them, other times snippets came up in conversations with friends or family, or something would happen to trigger them sharing a memory.

But here in Cabo Verde, being alone with my mother, sleeping in the same bed as her, seeing her dressing and undressing, combing her short hair, deciding what to wear, going to the hairdresser's and cutting her hair even shorter, walking around with her and spending so much time with her alone for the first time, I realize just how much our bodies grow apart. She doesn't look like other mothers. She is short, chubby, slow, her legs have a lot of varicose veins, cellulite, stretch marks, her breasts are big and droopy, her fingers are long and soft, her eyes shine when she laughs. Her body shows all the signs of the passing of time and of life.

Spending time alone with her, whether talking or in silence, watching her moving around, I come to appreciate and admire the beauty of her body again. I'm thirty-two years old, but it has taken us being here, removed from the regular life of Lisbon, far away from her kitchen and her home keeping and family-care duties, learning about the various different elements of her past, for me to see and understand my own marks and scars—products of my own life story but also marks and scars I've left on her life, on every layer of her body. Her body is the way it is because of me and my sisters. She always used to say, indeed she still says it, that I must study hard and work hard, because she doesn't want me to end up like her, *com a barriga encostada no fogão*—"with her belly forever pressed against the oven."

A sudden awareness of this beauty and learning comes to me one day after we've been sleeping, showering, dressing, walking, and undressing side by side in the same room for over two months. "Yes," I think, "her body is beautiful, and yes, it's full of sensuality."

It's a moment of simple but intense understanding, the realization that I can be needlessly insecure about my own body, ashamed of my own body even. It's strange to think about this because at home, throughout my childhood and through most of adulthood, we lived in the same home, shared rooms, shared beds, showered together, me and my sisters or our nieces. I even remember sharing the shower with my dad when I was a child. So where did all this shame and embarrassment about my own body come from? Why do I hide or cover myself so much? How did we grow up to become so distant from our own bodies? When did it start? What will it be like in the future? How will I see myself from now on? All these thoughts came to my mind that morning and stayed with me throughout the day. That night, seeing her undress again, I had a sudden feeling of being comfortable seeing her naked and not only that, a sudden feeling of being comfortable with own body too.

I suppose the routine of watching my mother dress and undress made me, albeit unconsciously, see the beauty in her transformations and realize that my own so-called imperfections and scars are really just markers in my life story. No wonder I've always said to my friends, with no sense of embarrassment, that for me there is no place more comfortable than mama's arms and, even though I'm thirty-two years old, I always like to climb into bed with her whenever I'm home.

It's never too late in life to make little discoveries like these, the beauty of bodies. Her body, my scars. I see my scars on her body, scars I don't remember making and scars that are still to come; scars that will be mine one day, but that she's carrying for me for now.

TWENTY-TWO

The hitch-hike

After visiting my auntie Nelita, we went to Gelo André to say farewell to Angelina. She's not expecting us because we haven't announced we're coming. My mother tells her that it's only right we come and bid her farewell because after all, she is her birth mother, and although she may not feel any great sense of friendship or love for her or between them, she feels no bitterness and wishes her well. Then my mother tells her that she's tracked down her dad, that she met her other family and is glad she did so. We are given our blessings and leave, or at least my mother does, I decide to stay with Angelina for a little longer. She remains silent, but eventually says, "I'm pleased to have met you both, I wasn't expecting that from life."

She walks around rearranging the tea towel, the chair, the table. She's nervous and I don't know quite what to do. She sits down and I can see she's shaking. Without looking at me, she says, "Go. I'm not going to show you to the door."

I get up and leave, unsure of what kind of turmoil I've left behind.

I thumbed lifts a lot in my youth, especially during summer holidays in the Alentejo where I would go with friends on archaeological summer camps. Until one day I had a serious accident jumping out of the back of a moving pick-up truck. The driver was drunk and thought it would be funny to scare us by not stopping where he was supposed to. We were all terrified and agreed to jump out when he stopped at the crossroads. With everyone screaming, I panicked and jumped too soon. I don't remember doing it and I was in the back of an ambulance by the time I came to. I spent the night in hospital with a concussion. I lost two teeth and ended up covered in bruises. I swore I'd never hitchhike again for the rest of my life. Even when someone I know well offers me a lift, I think twice before accepting.

Thumbing a lift with my mother was not, therefore, top of my agenda. However, the strangest things do happen.

We always knew that getting to and from Gelo André in a day was going to be difficult, but it was the only way we could fit it in and make sure we said goodbye to everyone. The problem is not so much the getting there but the getting back. It can be hard to find Hiaces running the Praia to Santiago route late in the day, especially if there's any kind of religious celebration taking place somewhere.

After saying our goodbyes, my mother and I head out to the road and wait for a van to pass. It takes a long time and when one finally does come it's packed to the rafters with the usual twenty-odd people crammed inside. No room for us, in other words. We prepare to wait again. I go for a pee behind a bush and when some kids come to splash around in the little stream beside the road, I go down to take some pictures and record the sound of them playing and chatting. But I do all this with my eyes and ears alert to the road. It starts to get dark and a cousin comes to stand and wait with us.

My mother is starting to get nervous. Gelo André is the last place on earth she wants to spend the night. Not because it doesn't have running water or electricity, but because it would mean staying at her mother's house.

More vans come and go, all of them full. Seeing my mother's growing concern, I start flagging down every passing car (there aren't that many) and asking for a lift. But they're all full, and the later it gets, the more tricky our situation becomes. I dare not look at my mother, for I know I'll be unable to hide my own sense of desperation. She, likewise, avoids looking at me, trying to hide her increasing despair behind a smile.

A car approaches and I wave for it to stop. All I can think of is getting us out of there and home. The car drives on, but then stops a little further ahead. I run to the car window and, doubtless sounding desperate, ask the two men inside if they're heading to Praia, begging them to give us a lift. They look at each other, shrug and nod for us to get in. We climb into the back and I start saying thank you, thank you, and trying to explain the scenario, but the two men don't say a word. The situation starts to feel strange, and I can't help thinking that it might have been better to stay where we were and spend the night in the village, no matter how awkward, rather than get into a car in the middle of nowhere in the dark with two strange men who are acting odd. Then I realize they're listening to the radio, following a Mass. This does nothing for my nerves: "Oh, my God," I think, "we've got into a car with some Catholic religious fundamentalists, we're doomed, this is the end!" I look at my mother and she looks back at me. She seems to be thinking the same thing, but we say not a word.

They keep quiet until the end of the radio prayers, when they make the sign of the cross. And then they suddenly start talking, apologizing for their earlier silence. They say we were lucky to get a lift at this time of night, that they only stopped because I was with my mother—they'd heard of cases where young girls thumb a lift, but as soon as the car pulls over the drivers are attacked and robbed by hidden accomplices.

My mother says it was God who sent them to us, and I find myself agreeing, I mean they were even listening to Mass on the radio!

My mother carries on chatting and says that one of them looks familiar. She says he reminds her of someone she knew as a child in Santa Catarina, and the man says his family is from there. He proceeds to talk us through his family tree, albeit omitting to mention the name of his grandparents. My mother, who has been tracking the names, asks if his grandparents aren't so and so. The man says, "Yes, they are!" Then my mother describes her family and, of course, the man knows Nho Armando

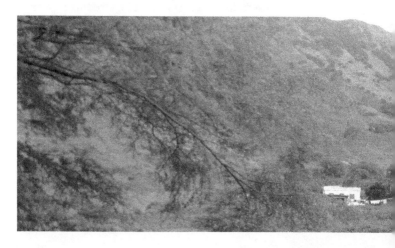

Polícia. As strange as it would seem, this man and my mother know each other's families, and quite possibly met as children.

I finally start to relax, and the conversation flows all the way to Praia. They want to take us all the way to Vila Nova and drop us at the door, "Cabo Verde is not what it used to be," one of them says, "you can't just walk home on your own nowadays."

But taking us all the way to our door is a little over the top, so I ask them to drop us by the bridge—there's a shortcut there that will have us home in five minutes.

"What are the chances?" I say as we set off walking, "I mean I know they say it's a small world, but Cabo Verde really is a tiny country!"

I start laughing as I remember the two of us standing in the dark by the road, trying to hide our growing sense of despair from one another. "Only you, Sónia," my mother says, "only you would have me hitchhiking for the first time in my life, at my age, out in the middle of nowhere."

TWENTY-THREE

Mantenhas para Casa

Not in my wildest dreams did I think my eighty-year-old grandfather might get married while I was in Cabo Verde. But that's what he told me he was going to do when I met him. "But why?" I asked him. He told me he wouldn't live much longer, and he wanted to marry Nána, the woman he'd been with for the past thirty years, in order to depart this world with a clean soul. The ease and familiarity with which people talk about death here is truly striking.

I asked him again what he meant, because he and Nána have actually been wed in a civil ceremony, why the need for a church wedding? "That's a matter between me and God," he replied, "He knows what I'm talking about."

So, I asked him where and when this wedding would take place, and he said it would likely have to be at home because he can no longer walk or stand for a long time. "Right," I said, "but surely the whole point of having this church wedding is that it's in the church, no? And don't you have enough sons and daughters and grandchildren to help you get there and back?" He smiled and said he'd let me know when the priest set a date.

It's funny talking to him and hearing stories about when he and my dad lived and worked together in Portugal, how their relationship was. He says my dad was a good son, a hard worker who cooked every meal for both of them; that he wasn't at all vain, but a humble young man. He tells me that when he decided to return to Cabo Verde my dad used to send him money to support the family, that he did this right until he stopped working himself. He also tells me that my dad bought a plot to build his own house in Cabo Verde, something I didn't know and am surprised to hear.

My grandfather has an amusing way of talking. He's old and not in good health, and so he always starts to talk very slowly. Then he stops and you think maybe he's dozed off, but then he suddenly starts talking again.

He was very pleased to meet my mother, even though she and my dad are no longer together.

My grandfather and Nána did indeed get married, but I missed it in the end. Not for want of trying, but because the priest simply passed by the house one day and announced that the ceremony would take place later that afternoon. It was around midday when he called and the bride-to-be wasn't even home. She was out in the countryside working in the fields. The only person who was at home, beside my grandfather, was one of my aunts. She had to arrange everything, from getting my grandfather dressed to sending word to her mother that she was to be married at five o'clock. There wasn't even time to arrange for a taxi. The bride had to stop what she was doing and walk who knows how many kilometers back along the main road, hoping a Hiace might pass. Meanwhile, my auntie summoned the witnesses, called the other siblings, and rushed out to buy rings.

From what I heard later, the bride arrived right at the last minute, wearing whatever clothes she had on, and the rings appeared at almost the exact moment the priest asked for them. Thus, they were declared man and wife!

While in Cabo Verde I got in the habit of saying *Até logo*, see you later, rather than *Até amanhã*, see you tomorrow. This is my mother's doing for she doesn't like "see you tomorrow," she says tomorrow is too far away and might never come—*O amanhã é muito longe!*

When I go to bid my grandfather farewell, he gives me two bottles of *grogu*, the traditional rum from the land—one for my dad and one for my uncle. He also gives me a message to pass on to my dad: "When you get home tell Fernando I'd like to see him again before I'm gone. Tell him that the love I've always had for him is the same as ever, I've no hard feelings towards him. Tell him that what destroyed our friendship were family intrigues, but that's all in the past now. Tell him my love for him is still the same!"

I ask for and am given his blessing: "May God protect you and your mother on your journey, all the way to your door." I say, "God bless you too," and "*Até logo.*"

TWENTY-FOUR

Together with the Freedom Fighters

I came to Cabo Verde with one very clear objective, my PhD project. My aim was to interview half-a-dozen people who participated in the liberation struggle in Guinea-Bissau, people who could talk about the struggle in general, but especially about the area of education.

I had a list of names of people I knew and others I'd come across in archival documents. I had no idea whether I'd be able to track them down, if they lived in Cabo Verde, or were even still alive. The names on my list were: Corsino Tolentino, Ana Maria Cabral, Maria da Luz Boal, Pedro Pires, Carmen Pereira, and Paula Fortes. If I managed to interview all six, I'd be very satisfied indeed.

I also initially intended to go to Guinea Bissau for a month, but soon realized there was more than enough for me to be getting on with in Cabo Verde.

The first email I sent was to Corsino Tolentino. I'd met him in Lisbon some years ago, so I contacted him before setting off for Cabo Verde explaining my project. His answer was immediate. He said that it was not only a great project but an urgent one and he pledged to help me any way he could!

He told me to contact the Fundação Amílcar Cabral and ask for Eng. Miguel Lima or Luisa Batista. I emailed them, outlining the project and my plans for when I was in Cabo Verde. I received a very prompt reply saying I'd be most welcome to call in and see them when I got to Cabo Verde.

And so, after the family marathon of the first few days, I went off to meet Miguel Lima. I showed him my list of six people, and he showed me his list of twelve people—my mission had doubled in size from one minute to the next. Not only that, his twelve were prominent figures in Cabo Verdean history. Furthermore, the foundation would afford me open access to their archives, the original documents.

I must say, all this left me a bit giddy. To get my hands on these original documents was one thing, but to then see how quickly and positively the dozen potential interviewees responded to my emails and phone calls was really quite something. It was essentially just a matter of suggesting a time and place to meet.

I threw myself into my research at the Fundação Amílcar Cabral, anxious not to turn up unprepared for the interviews, desperate to come across as professional, rather than a child meeting her heroes, which is how I felt—some of these people were like film stars to me.

I'd read so much of Cabral's writings but heard little about the liberation war itself, at least not from people who'd taken part in it. I was so excited to meet some of them because, when all's said and done, the opportunities I've had in life all resulted from that struggle. I'm a product of that struggle—it might sound pretentious or naff, but it's true.

One of my interviewees is Lilica Boal, Director of the PAIGC's main school, Escola Piloto. Curiously enough, I've known her name since childhood. My mother knows her too, for her cousin was a very close neighbor of ours in Reboleira, a woman named Tchucha. I remember Lilica Boal coming to visit Tchucha one day. The whole street stopped what it was doing and came out to see her. I remember a lady getting out of a very big car and going into my neighbor's house, and my mother saying she was a very important person in Cabo Verde. When I read out the names on my list to my mother, she reminds me of this earlier encounter with Lilica Boal.

When I meet my interviewees and introduce myself, I can tell they're shocked to see me—indeed they tell me so afterwards. Firstly, they're expecting a much older person. Secondly, having described myself in my email as Portuguese, they're expecting a white woman.

Well, thankfully it looks like things in the research world are changing! The people I interview are not only generous with their time, but welcome me into their homes, and share their personal archives with me. Commander and Chief Agnelo Dantas, for example, shows me the diary he kept during the war, something he says he's shown to very few people. Doctor Manuel Boal entrusts me with his collection of photographic slides from 1974; I will take them back to Germany and have them digitalized, then send the originals back to him. After all, he's been carrying them around for over forty years now, unable to develop or print them.

Amélia Araújo, the PAIGC radio operator and announcer promises to ask her daughter to help find a way to transfer an old vinyl the PAIGC produced—"*Uma cartucheira cheia de canções*," "cartridge belt of songs"—onto disc. I don't know how they manage it, but on the day of my departure, someone from the radio comes and presents me with a copy of the record on CD. In return, Araújo says that if I ever do make it to Guinea Bissau, she'd like me to go to the national radio headquarters and make copies of her old PAIGC radio program. She says it's been years since she last heard her voice on the radio.

I can't find any pictures of the Escola Piloto boarding school, so I'm forced to rely on the imaginary layout I make up in my head, based on descriptions in the interviews. It's frustrating, but then I'm presented with a map that some of my interviewees have worked on together in secret. Luisa Batista, Lilica Boal and a few former students, including her own son and daughter, got together to sketch out a map of the school. I'm given a first, and then a second draft, and it's really impressive.

I even get the opportunity to talk to one of Amílcar Cabral's daughters, Iva Cabral, who looks at me almost perplexed. "How did you come up with this topic?" she asks me, "This was the entire basis of my father's struggle!" She even agrees with me when I criticize the way academic studies of the Liberation War focus too much on her father, or on PAIGC policy, or the military side of things. She gives my project her full support.

Ana Maria Cabral asks me to have lunch with her the morning after I interview her. That same day, I got an email from Corsino Tolentino inviting me and my mother over for lunch at his place.

Talking to these people is an amazing experience. Each interview is a real education, a life lesson that gives me a much better understanding of my work. I soon see that I have a very limited idea of what the liberation struggle was, and a rather romantic one at that. But not only me, I see that the same might be said of others who admire what the PAIGC achieved.

My interviewees also confess their sadness over the current situation in Guinea-Bissau: "How can a land we gave our lives to end up in circumstances like this!"

Although I see them as heroes, they say they are not; they are just people, common people of the daily life, who did what they had to do according to the times they lived through. To paraphrase Pedro Pires in his interview, and that according to him, it is our generation to continue the struggle, as every generation has their own struggles. This may very well be true, and perhaps it is more a question of us, my generation, needing to have them as heroes. But I must say, no matter how much my generation likes to talk about revolution and struggle, I cannot imagine us giving up even half the material comforts they did. "We just closed the door and left all our possessions and lives behind in order to pursue a different dream!" That's the way Lilica Boal expressed to me, her joining the liberation struggle.

For me, it's just sad that the Cabo Verdean government seems determined to erase the legacy Cabral and others left us. He hardly even gets a mention at school. It's also sad to learn that most of the people I interview are unknown to most people of my generation in Cabo Verde, and to find out that there are plans to build a shopping mall where the Cabral monument currently stands. From what I hear, the plan is for the Cabral statue to serve as the entrance to the shopping center. What more is there to say?

The supportive environment at the foundation and the enthusiasm they show me, calling me to find out how

I'm getting on or to pass on some new bit of information, to invite me to lunch or let me know about some event, the way they give up their time for me, is nevertheless reassuring. They even take me to places I need to go sometimes, sit down with me and share their personal stories, make me feel like part of a big family. I, therefore, get the sense that, despite all the contradictions and political issues and disagreements, the PAIGC is somehow still a family. I feel like I've been adopted by them, like I'm their new granddaughter.

I end up interviewing fourteen people. They insist that I must come back and interview their comrades on other islands. I tell them I'll see what I can do.

On October 7, I invite all my interviewees to a meeting. I want to present them with the first results of my research and talk them through the next steps I plan to take. Four of them are away, but ten of them come. Eng. Miguel Lima is also present, as well as an uncle and a colleague. My mother asks to come too, she says it will make her very proud to watch me present my work.

I'm nervous, very nervous. The only comparable feeling I can think of is my first day at school. My mother took me and I remember being outside the school with the other parents and meeting my future teacher, Miss Fátima. She called my name and led me to the door, politely asked me to enter. This is the image I have in my head, along with a unique and indescribable smell, the smell of my first day at school, perhaps the only smell in my bank of memories.

I start the presentation, but the projector's not working so I have to use my laptop instead. When I get to the last two or three slides, my eyes start to well up and my voice begins to fail. I try to get a grip, but the tears start to fall and I lose control, I can barely talk. Oh my God, I feel so ashamed, I'm being completely unprofessional. But things get worse when the others start praising my project, my hard work and enthusiasm, my methodology, even my professionalism, saying that I helped them to see the value of their own work and gave them the opportunity to talk about something they thought nobody was interested in anymore, especially not people as young as me. There is no time for a last group photo. Everybody has to rush off because there's some kind of inauguration at the Pedro Pires Institute. I'm so touched that they made time for my presentation even though they had a prior engagement, that I start crying again.

Afterwards Luisa Batista tells me that I wasn't the only one in the room crying, just some people are better at hiding it than others. I received affirmation of this from Comander Agnelo Pereira Dantas too when sharing some pages of his diary and memories of the schools he saw in the liberated areas. He wrote to me at the end of the email, *"Sónia, continua a chorar, pois nos também choramos muito. . . na época. . . "* ["Sónia, keep crying, because we cried a lot too. . . during those times. . . "] of the liberation struggle.

TWENTY-FIVE

Departures

It's my last day in Cabo Verde and I run around like crazy. I've promised myself an hour on Prainha Beach, but first I have to go to the Amílcar Cabral Foundation, twice, then to the market, to Eugénio Lima to say "See you later" to my aunties and grandmother, and to receive their blessings.

There's no time to stop and think, but I eventually make it to the beach and enjoy a quiet moment and a dip in the warm water. The sea here bears no resemblance to the cold water in Portugal. Besides, here they have to make a distinction when referring to the beach. Praia means beach, so you say Praia when referring to the city, but *praia di mar* [beach of the sea] when referring to the beach. As a child in Portugal our parents would always say "beach of the sea" instead of "beach," which we always thought ridiculous. But now I've done it myself and completely understand it.

I think about the trip, how much I've enjoyed it without having properly digested it yet. When people ask me if I would like to stay and live here, I say no. Which is true, I don't see myself living in Cabo Verde for the foreseeable future, but maybe one day. I will certainly be back, hopefully with my dad next time.

My mother and I never did have those big conversations I was expecting us to have, nor did I ask her the questions I'd always wanted to ask, or even talk very much about myself. But she's speaking much more freely about her past in Cabo Verde now. She's also talking about issues that had become almost taboo back home, like my sister Fernanda, who died when she was just a few months old.

My mum knows more about me than I realized, and is very proud of my work and achievements. I saw this every time she introduced herself by saying "I'm here with my daughter who's conducting research for a PhD she's doing in Germany!" This was usually followed by an explanation, in her own words, of what my PhD entailed.

She remains very happy, a sort of happiness, or bodily and spiritual peace, that I haven't seen in her before. We haven't spoken much about how the trip has been going while we've been here, the same way we didn't discuss her hopes and expectations when I first invited her to join me. But looking back and thinking about it now, it's clear she'd been plotting and preparing for this trip for years. Way before the invite, she knew exactly what she would do if she got to go back to Cabo Verde.

My mother sometimes says there's a guardian angel watching over us, and in fact her final words to me before I head back to Berlin are *Anjo da guarda t'acompanhau* [May the guardian angel be always with you].

I decide to tell her about the lights I saw the day we went to her father's house for the first time. But it's hard to know how to explain it, so I just say I saw some lights one morning. The first thing she says is, "The Virgin Mary was with us!" I say, "No, mama, I just saw some lights hovering over you the day we went to your father's house." She remains silent for a moment, but then says,

"So then it was my father, he came to see me. To see what he could not see during his life."

She sometimes likes to say that there is a hand and a voice that forever guides us. I usually don't pay this any attention, but I have to say that out here in Cabo Verde it has often felt like a secret hand or voice was near.

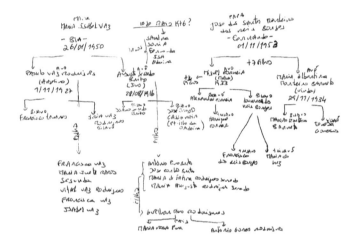

TWENTY-SIX

An abiding memory:
Santiago – Pedra Badejo

An abiding memory: Walking around Cabo Verde under a burning sun—we need an umbrella! Luckily, we've bought two. One green, one pink. We go to spend the day in Santiago—Pedra Badejo, and on the way there my mother sees her brother, Vital, out of the Hiace window, working away in a banana field. She tells me the field used to be a lot bigger, that it provided bananas to all the islands and beyond. We walk around the town, pass the church and at the top of the hill she tells me that the houses we can see down by the sea is Calheta. We continue on, and when we pass the Katchás statue she bursts into song, *Ah! Bulimundo, Bulim, Buliu*. We walk down to the black sandy beach, it's my first time seeing black sand. It's very hot. We spread a cloth out on the sand and sit down, all the while holding on to our open umbrellas.

Later we walk along the water's edge and I realize she's afraid, even though there are no waves and everything seems quiet and calm. She holds my hand and every time she senses we're getting in too deep she tugs me back towards the shore. Very calmly she says what she always said when we go to the beach: she tells me to respect the sea [*pamodi Mar, ka ten kau di pega*], because the sea has no place to grab.

TWENTY-SEVEN

Unwelcome travel companions

We're back in Lisbon, my last stop before heading back to Berlin. But first I need to see a doctor. Towards the end of our stay in Cabo Verde, on the third or fourth last night, there was a fly in our room that we couldn't get out. It was a green fly and, no matter how hard we tried, we just couldn't shoo the damn thing out of the room. So, we gave up, deciding that the worst it could do would be to disturb our sleep with its buzzing.

The next day we went to have lunch in Eugénio Lima at my uncle's house. I felt odd and ate very little, and then I got diarrhea and went for a lie down on my cousin's bed. My mother found this strange and said so to my uncle, "The girl is usually so picky about where she sleeps, she never goes for a nap in another person's house." "She's probably just tired," my uncle said.

The next day I was feeling much better, but some pimples had appeared on my left buttock. "Maybe some insect bit you," my mother said: "You see, that will teach you for always sitting on the floor!"

By the next day, our last in Cabo Verde, the pimples had become boils. My mother made me go to the neighbor's house for her to take a look. So, there I am showing my backside to an old lady and having her press my boils saying, "It might be from *bitchú*, but it's not moving so it's probably just an insect bite."

In the afternoon I took myself off to the beach, to say goodbye to the sea and thank the spirits that had watched over us during our stay. When I got back to the house my auntie was there, having come to say "see you later" and wish us a safe journey. My mother insisted on me showing my auntie my boils. She looked and looked, and then told me to turn my backside to face the sun so she could get a better look. Then she decided to rub spit on my boils to see if there was a reaction. How disgusting! I thought, do I really have to go through all this just because of a few boils?

"I thought it might have been *bitchú*," she said, "but it's not because they're not moving. You could go to the hospital, they'd be sure to know what it is, but as you're leaving tomorrow you might as well wait and go and see the doctor in Portugal."

We flew at night and I struggled to sleep because the boils had grown in size and started to itch. It became painful to put weight on my left buttock, which made the entire journey really uncomfortable. As soon as we got home, I made an emergency appointment with the doctor.

I explain the situation to the doctor and she sends me off to do a bunch of tests, because by now the boils have started to develop a white head. She calls another doctor in to take a look, and then she says, "These sorts of boils are very common in patients with HIV." And my world suddenly collapses. "HIV, what are you talking about?" I say, "I just arrived back from an African country, surely it's some kind of insect bite?" But they don't seem to take my travels into consideration. Instead, I'm subjected to a series of questions about my sexual life. I can see them doubting my answers, and then I start to doubt myself too. I've always been careful, haven't I?

They send me home with some creams to rub on my backside. All the next day I cannot sit, just lie. I eat very badly because I'm so anxious about the conversation I had with the doctor, a conversation I do not share with my mother. How could I share a thing like that after such an amazing trip?

At night the pain gets even worse. I look like I've had sharp needles prodded in my bum. I cry and scream with pain all night, gripping my mother's bed, my sister spreading more cream on my boils while my mother desperately tries to wake a neighbor up to see if he can take me to hospital. As the only one in the house with a driver's license, it's usually me taking others to the hospital.

Somehow, I manage to get to sleep and the pain eases off somewhat the next day. Night comes around again and I'm lying on the couch waiting for my sister to spread another layer of cream. We're all watching TV and talking, when suddenly my sister jumps up in terror, screaming for my mum to come fast. "Oh my God," I think, "what's happened, do they really look that bad?"

My mother comes rushing in from the kitchen and my sister starts yelling, "It's moving, they're all moving, I saw something coming out from inside the boil!" My mother moves in close to inspect my buttock, then she tells my sister to get Filomena, our neighbor, "Tell her to come quick!" She is quick and she's soon scrutinizing my buttocks too, and then she yells, "It's *bitchú*, yep, it's definitely *bitchú*!"

Yes, that stupid green fly that refused to leave our room in Cabo Verde laid some eggs in my backside, eleven to be precise. In Creole the fly is known as *Moska bota bitchú*. They took a week to develop into larvae, growing inside me, the host, and feeding on my tissue. The excruciating, needle-like pain I felt was because they were coming out to breathe, but my sister was covering their breathing hole with cream.

There are many different ways to get them out. You can put a piece of meat on top of the boil and wait for the larvae to move into this new piece of flesh, but the process can take days. You can go to hospital and have a nurse take them out. Or you can do it Cabo Verdean style, pressing down on the boil until the larvae pokes its nose out, then pulling it out all the way. My mother and neighbor decide that this is the best option.

I lie on the couch holding onto the armrest while my mother presses down on my boils and Filomena fishes the *bitchú* out. My darling sister decides to film the whole thing and sends the video to my other sister. In total, I somehow "give birth" to nine larvae.

The next day I go back to the doctor's and tell them it's an emergency. When they ask me at reception to justify why, I show them a glass jar containing the larvae, which are still alive. "Because I took these out of my backside last night," I say. They send me straight through to see the doctor and she immediately calls for her colleague who'd provided the second opinion.

Now they do what they probably should have done in the first place: call the emergency number at the Tropical Diseases Institute. They make an appointment for me and tell me they've never seen anything like it.

I save the larvae in the jar for three more days and take it with me to the Tropical Diseases Institute. I'm told to lie down and show my backside again. I don't suppose my buttocks have had this much attention since I was a baby in nappies.

The doctor is amazed, not that I'd gotten *bitchú* in Cabo Verde, which is unusual, but not that unusual. No, he's amazed that my neighbor managed to pull them all out without them breaking. It can be quite dangerous to have a bit of broken *bitchú* stuck inside you.

He asks me if I still have the larvae and I show him the jar. Then he asks for permission to take a photo of my left buttock, so he can show it to his students. I tell him he might as well, after all there's a video of it making the rounds. Then he asks me if I want to leave the jar of larvae with him, so that he can dispose of them safely. I say fine, though I've no doubt he'll keep them for research. He says I'll be left with a few scars where the boils are, and he gives me another antibiotic cream to rub on them and make sure they don't get infected. We say our thank-yous and goodbyes, and then he says 'Cutaneous myiasis.'

"Huh?" I say.

"That's the scientific term for *bitchú*."

After paying 65 euros for my consultation, I go to the pharmacy to buy the cream. Then I stop off to eat a Pastel de Belém and go for a walk in the Garden Praça do Império of what is one of the most colonial landmarks in Lisbon.

Because today is my thirty-third birthday.

TWENTY-EIGHT

Ragás

A place to be embraced, protected, cared for, nurtured. *Ragás, ragóse, kole*, all three Kriol expressions mean the hollow between the waist and knees of a seated person. The lap. After spending our first months at the chest and shoulder, being breastfed, burped, and cradled, we graduate to the *ragás*. It is there that we're fed and comforted, told our first stories, have our cuts and bruises blown on and plastered; there that we're taught our first lessons and feel protected, where we laugh and cry, and maybe get spanked for misbehaving. We're free to leave, but we often stay there a while longer, resting our heads, and if you happen to have siblings, the *ragás* becomes a battleground, everyone's hotly disputed favorite spot.

But for me it was never the *ragás* per se, but a variation on the theme, for I used to love sitting in between my mother's legs. I'd sit on the floor in between her legs and let her comb my hair, smoothing it down with a mixture of lard and olive oil. This was the eighties, there wasn't the wide range of products for African hair you get in the shops everywhere today, and even if there had been I doubt we'd have been able to afford it.

Anyway, I would sit on the floor in between my mother's legs religiously every Sunday, after washing my hair in the bath, letting her do my hair for school the next day. She would comb it and braid it and sometimes secure it by rolling it around a homemade thread we called *cordon*.

Or I would sit there and have my head inspected for lice, especially in summer when going with my neighbors or cousins to the public swimming pool was one of the highlights of the holiday. Twenty *escudos* for a whole afternoon, even if I wasn't technically old enough to be allowed in.

I still sit on the floor in between my mother's legs every time I come home, not to have my hair combed anymore, because I don't have any hair, but for her to do her little fingers trick on my scalp that she calls *krutch*. "Do me *krutch*, mama" [*Mamã, fasê-m krutch*], I say, and she does it, pressing her thumb down in such a smooth and gentle way that, almost without you noticing, there's a click and then a warm and relaxing feeling sweeps all over your head.

Conversation always flows when I'm sitting on the floor like this, be it about the telenovela, what sort of day we've had, school, our dreams, our plans, life's thrills and spills.

I went on this trip with her in July 2013, without really giving much thought to what would happen. I just wanted her to visit her country again, and for me to do my field research. But the trip took on a life of its own. For this journey, which I call the journey of a lifetime because I can't imagine any future travel living up to it, I found my traveling soulmate in Bia d'Lulucha. I found myself being carried along in the *ragás* of a woman who was herself an adventurous traveller, an experienced and ambitious risk taker, a dreamer and a planner, an organier and an improviser, with a *Rabelado* soul, and so many other things besides. I saw her laugh and cry, but above all else, I saw her smile with a lightness I'd never seen before.

I saw her become not the mother I knew, but one that unfolded before my eyes, and in a very unique way. I learned to answer her sometimes with words and other times with silence or nods, and most of the time by simply not thinking about the questions that had eaten away at me all these years—who are you, Mamã? Who were you? Where do you want to go? Can I go with you?

Ten years have passed since that journey and since this journal was written, and in the intervening years we've done many different things, been to so many other places and even backpacked together.

Back then, when I wrote these pages, during and shortly after the trip, all I wanted was to be able to share them with family and friends whenever they asked us about our time in Cabo Verde, to have dates, places, photos, flight tickets, and other bits and pieces recorded and on hand. I wanted to have a reminder of that unforgettable journey, because sometimes memory plays tricks on us. It doesn't matter whether you're young or old. Memory has a special knack for sneaking off without asking our permission.

Reading through those pages from time to time, flicking through them or just looking at the pictures, or simply glancing up and seeing the orange notebook there on my bookshelf, I'm also reminded of other stories, episodes, experiences, dreams, and sensations that I had there but wasn't able to capture in words at the time. I've been geographically a long way from home for ten years now, since that trip, *na buska bida*, as a kind Cabo Verdean expression for emigration puts it, "seeking life," and that orange notebook on my shelf has been *kel ragás na nha ragás* [the lap in my lap].

ABOUT THE AUTHORS

Maria Isabel Vaz was born and raised in the municipality of Santa Catarina, Santiago Island, in Cabo Verde. She migrated to Portugal with all her family in 1972 during the colonial occupation in Cabo Verde and the PAIGC liberation struggle in Guinea Bissau. In Portugal she worked as a domestic worker, where she married and became a mother of five. A humble and caring woman with strong values and beliefs, she made sure to transmit her knowledges, life experience, and social justice principles to her daughters. Gardening and farming are her passions, an inheritance brought from her life in the countryside in Cabo Verde. Maria Isabel Vaz is now retired and lives in Amadora, Portugal.

Sónia Vaz Borges is a militant interdisciplinary historian and social political organizer. She received her PhD in History of Education from the Humboldt-Universität zu Berlin (HU). She is the author of *Militant Education, Liberation Struggle, Consciousness: The PAIGC Education in Guinea Bissau 1963–1978* (2019). As a result of her research Vaz Borges coauthored and codirected the short films, *Navigating the Pilot School* (2016) and *Mangrove School* (2022). Vaz Borges is also the author of *Na Pó Di Spéra. Percursos nos Bairros da Estrada Militar, de Santa Filo-*

mena e da Encosta Nascente (2014), and editor of the *Zines, Caderno Consciência e Resistência Negra* (2007–2011). Vaz Borges is Assistant Professor in the History and Africana Studies Program at Drexel University. Vaz Borges continues to write on education and liberation struggles and is working on her concept of the "walking archive."

ABOUT COMMON NOTIONS

Common Notions is a publishing house and programming platform that fosters new formulations of living autonomy. We aim to circulate timely reflections, clear critiques, and inspiring strategies that amplify movements for social justice.

Our publications trace a constellation of critical and visionary meditations on the organization of freedom. By any media necessary, we seek to nourish the imagination and generalize common notions about the creation of other worlds beyond state and capital. Inspired by various traditions of autonomism and liberation—in the US and internationally, historical and emerging from contemporary movements—our publications provide resources for a collective reading of struggles past, present, and to come.

Common Notions regularly collaborates with political collectives, militant authors, radical presses, and maverick designers around the world. Our political and aesthetic pursuits are dreamed and realized with Antumbra Designs.

www.commonnotions.org
info@commonnotions.org

BECOME A COMMON NOTIONS
MONTHLY SUSTAINER

These are decisive times ripe with challenges and possibility, heartache, and beautiful inspiration. More than ever, we need timely reflections, clear critiques, and inspiring strategies that can help movements for social justice grow and transform society.

Help us amplify those words, deeds, and dreams that our liberation movements, and our worlds, so urgently need.

Movements are sustained by people like you, whose fugitive words, deeds, and dreams bend against the world of domination and exploitation.

For collective imagination, dedicated practices of love and study, and organized acts of freedom.
By any media necessary.
With your love and support.

Monthly sustainers start at $15.

commonnotions.org/sustain